TEXAS RATTLESNAKE

By Scott Edelman
Published by Ballantine Books

WARRIOR QUEEN: The Totally Unauthorized Story of Joanie Laurer
TEXAS RATTLESNAKE: The Unfiltered, Completely Unauthorized Story of Steve Austin

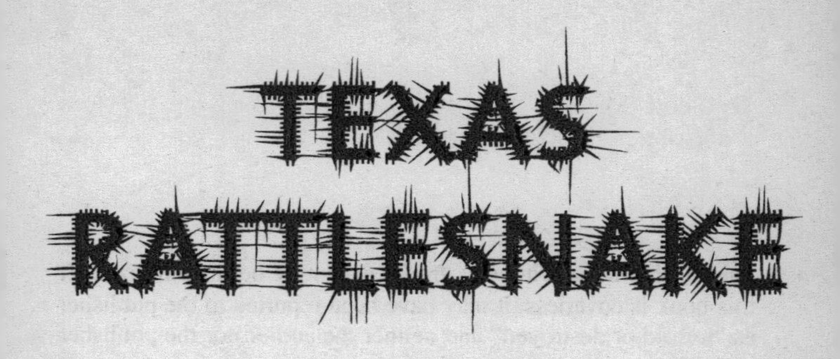

Scott Edelman

BALLANTINE BOOKS • NEW YORK

A Ballantine Book
Published by The Ballantine Publishing Group
 Published in the United States by The Ballantine Publishing Group, a division of Random House, Inc., New York, and simultaneously in Canada by Random House of Canada Limited, Toronto.

www.randomhouse.com/BB/

Library of Congress Catalog Card Number: 00-190321

ISBN 0-345-44146-X

Manufactured in the United States of America

First Edition: May 2000

10 9 8 7 6 5 4 3 2 1

Acknowledgments

Special thanks must go to the following core members of my own federation, without whom this book could not possibly have been wrestled into reality:

Joe Varda, for being the "Stone Cold" Steve Austin to my own Mankind; Barry Malzberg, for showing that it was possible to do the impossible, and better than I ever could; Lee Edelman, for all those years spent hard-core wrestling in our parents' apartments; Jeff Eisenberg, Michael Lano, Tom Miller, Al Ortega, and Sue Schneider for keeping things in focus; Trevor Vartanoff, for his impressive photographic memory; Barney and Toni Edelman, the tag-team champions of Florida; David Bischoff, for introducing me to Winchell Dredge; Irene Vartanoff, who gave the Stone Cold Stunner to my heart; Kirk Poland, who surely could have done it better and faster; my grandfather Nathan Goldstein, the former

Brooklyn bookie, who must have planted wrestling in my genes and is laughing in the great gambling den in the sky; Mark Hintz and Carl Gnam, for saying "No" and then being gracious enough to say "Yes." Finally, most of all, thanks must go to Steve Williams, who reinvented himself as "Stone Cold" Steve Austin and remade the face of modern professional wrestling.

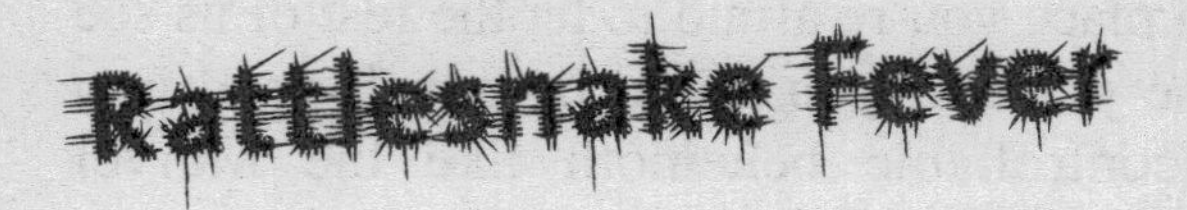

chapter 1

Did you ever have the urge to tell off the boss? Have you ever wanted to advise the suits in the corner office to get stuffed? Perhaps you've even yearned to pop a few brewskis, toss them back fast, and then wave your middle finger in the face of the big kahuna who signs your paycheck, all at the same time.

Come on. Be honest. After all, it's just you, me, and Steve Austin here.

Most of you would say yes, that you're tired of toeing the line for chump change while the Big Man rakes in all the bucks. Whether working the assembly line or pushing pixels in some high-tech, white collar Internet job, you're resentful of doing all the work and seeing little of the reward.

And as for that small fraction of you who say, "No, I've never felt that way," well, you see, the trouble is that the rest of us just don't believe you. No one could possibly be that pure and good. We know that somewhere deep inside you, in a secret, hidden place you're afraid to let the rest of us see because you fear you might be transformed into an uncontrollable behemoth like the Marvel Comics character the Incredible Hulk and never turn back; in some subterranean part of your being, you're as mad as hell as us other mortals, and given half a chance, you wouldn't take it anymore.

Then, man, do we have a role model for you.

If you're frustrated, there's a man who feels your pain.

If you're pissed off, there's an icon who makes your emotions seem inconsequential by comparison, because he's the most distressed dude on the planet.

If you think that *you* have it in for the powers-that-be, then step aside—there's a chrome-dome foul-mouth striding the world in jeans and a black vest who burns with a greater hatred for those in charge than you could ever possibly know.

He's a fearless son of a bitch who has no respect for authority. As he slugs down his beer—which had damn well better be American, or his white-hot temper will get the best of him—he's sure to let you know that he doesn't take crap from anyone. As he swaggers along the aisles of the world's largest arenas, which his popularity has caused to sell out, his toughness is undisputed. Facing the worst the wrestling world can throw at him, he takes no prisoners, delivering the goods to pull triumph out of defeat in the face of adversity. His language is obscene, his mannerisms—particularly the middle fingers that he loves to display so often—are vulgar, and yet the more he swears, the more wrestling fans swear by him.

This ass-kicking Texan has caused a revolution in the stale world of sports entertainment, but ask this growling cowboy and he'll tell you that he doesn't give a damn about that—he just wants to raise a little hell. There's nothing he likes better than sticking it to the Man, and he is the spiritual inspiration for every blue-collar worker who can't—and for any white-collar worker as well.

He may very well be the meanest dude the wrestling world has ever known.

The name of this incorrigible brawler? This dyed-in-the-wool rabble-rouser may have been born Steven Williams, but you know him best as "Stone Cold" Steve Austin, also known as the "Rattlesnake," the man who rejuvenated professional wrestling in the nineties.

And that's the bottom line.

Why? If you've been paying any attention, you'll know the reason why.

'Cause "Stone Cold" said so.

Steve Austin has tried to sum up the reasons for his broad appeal, and his suggested answer for his success is a simple one. He has said, "I guess people can identify with me because I am in real life exactly what you see on TV." Yes, that's always been a part of any grappler's success, that good match between the character's mask of personality and the wrestler's soul. Fans can tell when a wrestler is faking it or slightly ashamed of his role, and so things will fail to click with the audience and he'll soon be gone. But for Austin, it's more than that, really.

It's not just because his inner and outer selves are a good fit. It's because who he is so well represents who we are as a society at the dawning of a new millennium.

As you watched Austin give the Stone Cold Stunner to his defeated opponents, most of his audience has wished to do the same to those riding their own backs. When Austin bellows out "Hell, yeah!" who hasn't wished to grunt the same where it counted in their own lives?

If you like Steve Austin, if his rowdy act touches you in some way, what does that say about you?

It simply says that you're like most Americans, who are sick and tired of being sick and tired.

While we think about them from time to time, we no longer worry deeply about terrorists, politicians, or criminals. Even other wrestlers know who the real existential enemy of the twenty-first century is, for those of us leading lives of quiet desperation. It's the person who looks over our shoulders to make sure we're not taking too many bathroom breaks. "There is no horror now," said WWF wrestler Paul Levesque, known these days more widely as the untrustworthy Triple H. "To the average person, the real-life enemy is their boss." And no one more exemplifies that hatred of the boss than Austin. He has been able to tap into that undercurrent of dissatisfaction and rage in a way no wrestler has been allowed to do so before.

It isn't just the wrestlers who have come to realize this. Sociologists in the academic world—just the sort of highfalutin folks with whom Austin would love to get in a slobberknocker—have also noted a change in the weather. Alan Dundes, a professor of anthropology and folklore at the University of California at Berkeley, agrees that different times call for different wrestlers, because having our heroes in the ring beat up on cartoon characters based on the worst stereotypes from other countries just won't cut it anymore. "Since the end of the Cold War," he has said, "there's been no one for us to beat up on, no real hated enemy like we had with the Soviet Union for so many years. We've had a hard time finding outlets for our machismo."

And so the hunt for enemies in the wrestling world has turned inward, toward those who rile us as no others can. And also to those toward whom we must show some restraint, or lose our jobs. That's one of the beauties of the way the "Stone Cold" Steve Austin character was conceived. If we opened a can of whup-ass on our bosses the way Austin has on his on a daily basis, we'd be in jail.

But by pulling that same routine, Austin has climbed to the top of the game, and even with injuries from time to time taking him away from us, he stays there still.

Once in a great while a wrestler comes along who defines his generation. Where other wrestlers appeal just to the cognoscenti, this rare breed appeals even to those who are not wrestling fans and brings a larger audience on board.

At the birth of television, Gorgeous George was such a man. And by Gorgeous George we do not mean the voluptuous blond still wrestling today who has borrowed the great one's name. No, we mean the effete grappler from the fifties who entered the ring along a path of strewn rose petals. With his bizarre antics, such as spraying the ring with perfume to make it suitable for his refined senses, he captured a public's imagination and sold more televisions than RCA. He became a star, as popular a figure in that time as Howdy Doody or Milton Berle, and brought wrestling into America's living rooms.

The sport would have to wait three decades to see another of his like.

In the eighties, unexpectedly, it was the comic book hero Hulk Hogan, who told the kids to eat their vitamins so they could grow up to be good, strong Americans. It was a simpler time, and for a generation of fans of the squared circle, he defined wrestling. He made those who cared little for the sport sit up and take notice. They tuned in and stayed to see the over-the-top activities of this genuine superstar. And when he used his skills to build a career in the movies and on television, fans followed him.

We are now privileged to live again in such a time, and the wrestler who defines us, who tells us what wrestling was like in the nineties and will be like in the new century beyond, is Steve Austin. Just as Hogan defined wrestling for his decade, Austin is the most recognizable name in the sport today.

But that's not the only common trait between these two men. It's more than just their popularity that makes them similar. Each was a catalyst without whom you probably would not be devoting your Monday nights to wrestling or reading this book today. Hogan and Austin both came into a moribund sport and turned it around when it needed it the most. They each reinvented professional wrestling in their own images, bringing it to new heights that were previously unimaginable. Hogan showed the world that wrestling was more than just fat men and big cigars. He announced that it was safe for kids, and the makeup of the audience immediately changed.

And Austin, too, sends out a message. Regardless of his prodigious talent on an individual level in the ring, it is instead this talent on a universal level that will be more important in the long run. It is Austin's ability to wrestle the sport itself to the next level that will be most important when the scribes a hundred years hence gather to assess his impact.

But there is a difference between the two men as well. For where Hogan used his hands to cup a hand around an ear and listen for the cheers of fans, Austin uses his hands to deliver an in-your-face middle finger to those he detests. And it is a middle finger that society is not very happy with, as can be seen by the fact that the center digits that we can see televised on Monday night *RAW* and the numerous pay-per-view events is pixilated out of existence as an act of censorship on Thursday night *SmackDown!*.

That Austin's fingers can disappear like that on a regular basis is indicative of the bizarre conflict that America is having wrestling with its own morals, and the central place that Austin occupies in that battle.

For though Austin is seen as a hero by most wrestling fans, outside of the fellowship of the squared circle there is fear over what kind of hero he has become. Once, only the good guys were cheered, leaving the bad guys to be soundly booed. But somewhere along the line the edges blurred. The heroes became the bad guys, untrustworthy for being as straight as arrows, and tagged with the epithet "old-fashioned." The bad guys got the huzzahs. The bad boys got the girls. The spot in our hearts once reserved only for the Lone Ranger has been kidnapped by the "Stone" Stranger.

Nowhere has this firestorm become more crystallized than with Steve Williams, the man who became Stone Cold Steve Austin, and who has become a lightning rod for comments about wrestling.

Some parents worry that their kids will grow up to be Steve Austin in real life, giving authority figures the finger and cursing out anyone who dares to cross them. On the stage of the ring, watching someone behave like that can be entertaining, but they know that if the children can't separate fantasy from reality, they'll end up in detention, in prison, or somewhere far worse.

So there are those who are worried about the mixed signals that we send as a culture, though it's very clear that we send them by choice. We both lap up the message and condemn it at the same time.

Society is very confused by wrestling at the moment. It both loves and hates it, making us at war with ourselves. Both of these conflicting emotions are in evidence with a passion and strength that is almost schizophrenic.

One the one hand, when the rating czars tally the success and failure of the product at week's end, cable wrestling events—both of the WWF and the WCW as well—are usually filling at least seven of the slots for top ten shows. But on the other hand, radio talk shows and Sunday morning political chat hours all bemoan the coarsening of our world, somehow managing to blame wrestling for all the ills of civilization.

You can't have it both ways. Love it or hate it, but make up your mind, pick one and stay with that.

But be careful with what you choose.

Wrestling is not a catalyst for social change. It never has been, except as an impetus for the sale of television sets. Wrestling is but a mirror held up to that society. And what we see when we peer into that mirror is our own faces looking back. Hating wrestling is akin to hating ourselves, which is about as self-defeating a philosophy as one can have.

If the world around you has changed, you shouldn't blame Stone Cold Steve Austin. Even fellow wrestler the Rock, whose ring persona as the "People's Champion" makes him one of the Rattlesnake's most ardent adversaries, comes to Austin's defense on that issue, placing the blame squarely where it belongs. "The parents are the ones allowing their kids to watch the WWF Monday nights," he has said. "The parents are the ones allowing their children to purchase the Stone Cold Steve Austin finger."

And the Rock, as anyone who's been paying attention to Austin's antics well knows, has seen the Steve Austin finger often. He's been on the receiving end of the gesture many times. One of the more amusing for viewers was at the Backlash pay-per-view event held in Providence, Rhode Island, on April 25, 1999, when the Rock got a little cocky about the way the bout was proceeding.

Having knocked Austin down with his famed Rock Bottom move, the Rock took over one of the ringside cameras and started fooling around, enjoying broadcasting images of the Rattlesnake's defeat. First he stood over the fallen Austin, who looked quite groggy and beaten. Then the Rock turned to focus his camera out to the crowd. When the People's Champion looked back to Austin with the lens, expecting to see his opponent still defeated, he was startled to instead focus on two middle fingers aimed in his direction. Shortly thereafter, the Rock lost the camera and felt the fury of the Stone Cold Stunner.

So when Rocky Maivia comes to Austin's defense as a wrestling icon, it speaks loudly.

Wrestlers frequently find themselves having to defend their sport to those who neither appreciate nor understand it. WWF owner Vince McMahon tried to do so when speaking on January 21, 1999, to the packed and hostile room of reporters at the Television Critics Association annual convention. He tried to explain what the modern day sport is all about to a crowd who, based on their questions and responses, didn't really want to listen.

"You have to think of us, really, as an action adventure," he told the group of wrestling outsiders. "The World Wrestling Federation is not about wrestling. It is an action adventure. It's a soap opera. There are elements of sitcom in the WWF. It's all about individuals who perform—these extraordinary athletes, these incredible athletes—and the charisma that they have is second to none on television today.

"The World Wrestling Federation is Hollywood. It's Broadway, maybe a little dash of Springer thrown in there, maybe some spare parts from the Roadrunner cartoons, maybe a plotline stolen, or borrowed, if you would, from *One Life to Live*. That's who we are. We really are entertainment. We're a hybrid of just about everything there is on television today. That's who the WWF is. It's really a hoot, when you get down to it. That's what it is, a hoot.

"No cue cards. No laugh tracks. It's the real deal. It's an opportunity for our audience—our television audience—to come to a live event and see what it is we do, to feel it, to feel that emotion that we bring, to be able to really have a good time, to experience that 'hoot' I'm talking about."

McMahon comes off as more reserved than Austin does when responding to people who question his chosen sport. Maybe he has to. After all, he's the CEO, and not just an employee with the flair for loose lips. But Steve Austin finds himself under no such restrictions. In talking on the same subject to *Sport* magazine, it sounded as if he were about to give the inquiring reporter a Stone Cold Stunner.

And if he had, we wouldn't have been surprised.

"To me," said Austin, speaking of those who belittle him and his career, "those people are extremely narrow-minded, uptight, and insecure. I bust my ass every night, and I challenge anybody in the world to get on the road with me for 250 days a year."

Sometimes, however, the barbs get aimed at Austin not just from those outside the sport, but from those inside as well.

For to some, what Austin does isn't wrestling—it's merely street fighting. (As if there has ever been a "mere" about anything that Austin has done.) Frank Krewda, regular writer of the "Krew-Cuts" column in *Pro Wrestling Illustrated* magazine, used his May 1999 column to nail Austin as the most overrated wrestler of the year.

But to most of the world, the distinction between grapplers and gut-punchers is meaningless. Many wrestling fans feel that if Austin isn't involved, then it just ain't wrestling. During each injury that has caused him to pause for recuperation, they've hungered for him to get back into the ring. During his various absences, brought on because he just can't listen to his body when it tells him to slow down, all the fans want is to see him come back and upset all that went on since he stepped away.

In 1999, Austin told *Cigar Aficionado* magazine that "I'm a corporate nightmare. I don't dress up a whole lot. Sometimes my language is a little offensive. I drink a few beers on TV. I'm not a yes-man. I do what I want, when and how I want." But based on the bottom line of dollars flowing in, he's no corporate nightmare—he's instead a corporation dream.

Austin is the true six million dollar man, because that's what his estimated income was for 1999, when salary, appearance fees, and merchandising licensing were factored in. His persona is popular around the world, setting up another disconnect between fantasy and reality.

In the real world, Austin's face would be on Wanted posters. But in McMahon's world, we're made to want his posters.

In just a few short years, Stone Cold Steve Austin has become perhaps the biggest draw of Vince McMahon's World Wrestling Federation. When the fledgling UPN began running *SmackDown!* on Thursday nights, it changed the fortunes of that upstart network. The suits whom Austin hates so much were startled. Their viewer statistics were changed as dramatically as anything that ever happened inside the ring. The number of men aged 18-34 watching UPN on Thursday nights went up 617 percent compared to the previous viewership, while the number of male teenagers tuning in increased by an incredible 1,367 percent! These are figures that broadcasters dream of, for where viewers come, advertisers follow.

In many ways, as much credit as must be given to Vince McMahon, Stone Cold Steve Austin must be counted as the man responsible for making this happen. He's the one the fans wanted to see. He's the one the fans want to *be*.

His merchandise outsells that of any other WWF wrestler. In fact, more Steve Austin merchandise has been sold than paraphernalia for any other wrestler in history. Equally remarkable is the time frame for all of this. It took Austin just a few short years to eclipse the mountain of merchandising that it took Hulk Hogan over a decade to unload. Additionally, more than half of the sports videos in the U.S. were created by the WWF, eclipsing baseball, hockey, boxing—even that formerly undisputed king, football—put together.

And when you browse the aisles at the video stores trying to decide just which tapes to buy or rent for your weekend entertainment, whose picture do you see glaring out at you? Why, Stone Cold Steve Austin's, of course. His face makes those cassettes leap into our hands, and marketers know and exploit this.

Why else would the USA Network structure its year 2000 Super Bowl half-time show around an Austin interview where the Rattlesnake let the world know of the extent of his latest injuries? Television executives know that viewers will pay more attention to Austin sitting calmly with a beer in hand than to any musical extravaganza that football can hope to throw at us.

Well, not *all* television executives.

After all, Steve Austin is one of the core reasons why the WWF is continually whipping the WCW in the ratings every Monday night. Yet it seems that Eric Bischoff, the brains behind WCW's bookings, let Austin slip out of his fingers when it had him locked to a contract. They just didn't think that Austin was going to amount to much.

They were wrong. Had Bischoff been a little smarter a few years back, the WCW might be on top of the wrestling world.

And at this time in wrestling's long history, Austin is indisputably on top of the game.

When the readers of *Rampage* magazine were asked to voice their opinion for the greatest wrestler currently active, Steve Austin received 36 percent of the vote (followed by the Rock with 23 percent and Hulk Hogan with 10 percent). In the same poll, readers were also asked to name who would still be left standing in a three-way brawl among Austin, the WCW's Goldberg, and the then-ECW Taz (who has since moved on to the WWF himself). So undeniable is the man's prowess that a full 50 percent of voters said Austin would be the inevitable winner of such a fight.

Austin has so dominated the wrestling world that the editors of *Pro Wrestling Illustrated* magazine named him number one on their prestigious Top 500 list not only in 1998, but in 1999 as well. So impressed were these experts by Austin's talents and popularity that this was only the second time in history that a wrestler had captured the top slot in two consecutive rankings. Austin ranked third in 1997, but even with his injuries, he seems on the verge of pulling number one out of his hat yet again. (By the way, Bret Hart is the only one who ever did it before, back in 1993 and 1994.)

Austin, of course, as befits his barbed-wire personality, was not gracious about the honor. In fact, he was downright aggressive. "Don't get me wrong," he told the editors. "I appreciate the fact that I was named the number-one wrestler in the entire world. But it's not like you guys went out on a limb for me. Who the hell else could you have picked? Don't come around expecting a pat on the back for the only thing your magazine could have done."

Prideful words, and in sentences a little rough around the edges. Coming from anyone else, they'd be seen as boastful. But springing out of the mouth of Austin, they're nothing but the truth.

He's right. Who else is there? At the pinnacle, he seems to stand alone. Austin has even become so accepted by the mainstream that he is the first wrestler chosen to be a part of the American Dairy Association's prestigious "Got Milk?" campaign, following up such sports figures as Cal Ripken, Jr. and Mark McGwire. He was seen plastered in top magazines across the country, sporting a milk moustache and proclaiming: "It better be ice cold for Stone Cold."

He's gotten so darn respectable that the A&E cable channel devoted an hour to delving into his life.

And these are not the only venues not traditionally associated with wrestling that have paid attention to the Rattlesnake. On the Fox Teen Choice Awards on August 12, 1999, Austin was named Choice Pro Wrestler and given a surfboard as an award.

His long years of hard work have finally borne fruit. And not just for himself, but for us as well. For Austin's acceptance into the mainstream is wrestling's acceptance, too. It allows lovers of the sport to stop being excluded, as they have been for so long.

Pat Patterson, long affiliated with the WWF, has said: "Austin is a man who has a lot of guts and doesn't try to play games with anyone the way Vince and Shane do. He's a great ambassador for the WWF."

But it's more than that. By vaulting to the next level of popularity, Austin does far more than just act as the public face of the WWF—he acts as the current ambassador to the world for the entire sport of wrestling, elevating it from its previous cult marginalization to mainstream blockbuster status, telling the naysayers that we're here, and they'd better get used to it.

His road from nonentity to superstar status was not an easy one. He has fought and survived more battles than most armies put together. But this Energizer Bunny of wrestling just won't stop. "They tell me where to defend the belt and I'm there," he has said. "Other than that, it doesn't matter if we're wrestling in front of five people at a garbage dump. It's all the same to me."

"Austin 3:16," the catchphrase that made

Austin the man he is today, says "I just whupped your ass."

But somehow, at the same time, he also "whupped" our hearts and minds.

chapter 2

Texas Tornado

The state of Texas is known for many large and powerful things. First of all, its immense size—its 267,277 square miles make it the second largest state in the lower forty-eight, coming in right behind its fierce rival California, though you won't get very far in the Lone Star State trying to tell a Texan that he is second-best at anything. Texas boasts the Alamo, which we are often urged to remember, a battle site made so famous over time that people seem to forget it is most famous for having been a lost cause. Also famous, which Texans would rather forget about, is that the state is also the site of an assassination that changed the course of a country, and the Texas Book Depository that housed Lee Harvey Oswald is one of its top tourist attractions. Texas brought us President Lyndon Johnson, one of the nation's greatest political minds, and also the famed Dallas Cowboy Cheerleaders, some of the greatest bodies as well.

But there is one other event not usually recounted in this book of deeds that might someday eclipse all the others, causing them to be as forgotten and anonymous as Texas tumbleweeds. And that is that Texas was the birthplace and molding influence of little Steven Williams, the boy who would eventually reinvent himself as the man we know today as Stone Cold Steve Austin. Steven Williams was born December 18, 1964, in the city of Austin, Texas—with the name of his hometown claimed today as making no difference toward his eventual choice of moniker. That was just one of life's many coincidences.

The man who came to be known as Stone Cold Steve Austin is proud to be a child of the state he was born in. Texas is so much a part of Austin, so deeply at home within his heart, that he has taken decisive action (as all Austin's actions are) to make sure the world knows of this devotion—he has had the shape of the state itself tattooed on his left calf. The large impression emblazoned on his skin shows the outline of the state in bright red, with the head of a steer emblazoned across it. No one looking at the man could ever deny that he was Texas born and Texas bred.

Williams has gone through three last names in his life, and in fact was actually born as Steven Anderson. But since Austin barely has any memories of the man who gave him that name (the man with whom he shares his genes left before the boy could really get to know him), "Williams" has always been the answer given when people ask for the name behind the Rattlesnake. The Williams name that he quickly came to carry originated with his mother's second husband, and that's how Austin thinks of himself when he isn't being Stone Cold Steve Austin. If you peeked at his financial records, which you couldn't get near without risking a Stunner, that's the name you'd see.

His mid-December birth date gives him the astrological sign of Sagittarius.

It would be useful to see how Williams compares with the supposed attributes of this sign of the zodiac. Many deny the influence of the stars, but as for Williams, well, let's see.

According to the experts who know best, Sagittarians are a freedom-loving bunch, who bristle under the heel of authority. They are straightforward in their interactions with others. They don't pussyfoot around. You always know where you stand with them. What's on their minds is quickly on their lips, and you'll have no doubt about what they think. They enjoy traveling, so it's a good idea if they end up with a chosen career that requires it. It would not be a good match for a Sagittarian to end up behind a desk.

Given a choice, a Sagittarian is on the side of the underdog. They burn to correct the injustice in the world. If not given a choice, and they're backed into a corner, they'll turn rebellious and strong-willed in the pursuit of what they think is right.

Their tempers are short ones. They often flare up over incidents that others would consider trifles, demonstrating a stony impatience with the needs and desires of others. In the workplace their behavior can therefore be seen as inconsiderate and domineering, for in that arena they often interact with others in a manner that is both boastful and vulgar.

In making their life choices, Sagittarians often end up in risky lines of work, or as sportsmen who indulge in dangerous pursuits. Those born under this sign can find themselves the recipients of dreadful accidents and injuries occurring from just those activities.

Is any of this beginning to sound like someone familiar? It sounds like a snapshot of a man we have come to know very well.

Austin is about as far from a corporate man as one can get in this world. His manner is gruff, his demeanor, unforgiving. You know just what he thinks of you, because "Stone Cold" said so. His constant run-ins with boss man Vince McMahon are the cornerstone of his career, and one of the reasons for his worldwide fame. Austin has carved a career as a risk taker, experiencing many unavoidable injuries—injuries that have drawn as much attention as his triumphs—due to the nature of the explosive field of battle he has chosen.

With all of this starry evidence etching out his personality, how could Steven Williams have turned out as anything else? Looking backward from the pinnacle of today, it seems to have been unavoidable. He seems to have ended up where the stars required.

Neither his parents nor siblings—Williams was the middle child of three—foresaw the road he would walk, though perhaps they could have, if only they had read the signs. And not just the astrological signs, about which there is great debate regarding their meaning and accuracy, but also the intense interest Steve Williams began to pay to a particular type of television programming as a child.

He was always an avid wrestling fan, from the moment he discovered that there was such a thing. He started watching the athletic competitions when he was in the fifth grade. This newfound hobby was not so well-received by his parents. His family would continually try to get him to turn off the set and seek out other pursuits, which happens to be a truism of many children who turned out to be future wrestlers (so parents, perhaps you should learn to let the kids alone, as banning the sport only seems to increase the interest in it). But Steve paid them no mind. His interest in wrestling continued. He kept drinking it in, dazzled by the new world he had discovered.

The fairy-tale world of clean-cut comic book heroes and snarling over-the-top melodramatic villains was just too good for young Steve to resist. While his parents were riding him to go outside and do something a little more active with his time, he'd while away the hours watching Paul Boesch's *Houston Wrestling* on the tube. It was magnetic. At the time, he was like all young children, and believed every word of it and every action to be 100 percent real. If a wrestling insider had told him that the grunting, grappling men who seemed to hate each other so much were actually friendly business acquaintances behind-the-scenes who decided in advance who would win and who would lose, young Steve Williams would have been shocked.

If Stone Cold Steve Austin could somehow get himself a time machine and go back to sit beside the boy he once was, and tell him the many secrets he has since learned, it's still doubtful that the kid would have given up his illusions.

Austin remembers fondly these childhood times back in South Texas, and has no reticence in talking about them. In an interview with Chris Heath of *Rolling Stone*, Austin explained that he was not much different from the other kids growing up in his neighborhood. "We were pretty damn ordinary kids," he said. "We just ran around on the street, went to school, did normal stuff. Got in our share of trouble."

And yet the "trouble" he speaks of really didn't amount to much when compared to the sort of drama that happens to him now that he leads a life in the ring. In fact, those who know him only from his image today might not recognize the picture put together by those who knew him best back then. Quite the opposite of his modern day public persona, he was considered a nice, rather shy kid who was always polite—nothing at all like the hell-raising Rattlesnake he would one day be. Steve Williams was a well-regarded boy and then young man who went out of his way to please his peers and teachers. He was known for his wide smile rather than his growl, and his long blond hair rather than his shaved head.

So even though he was engrossed in the on-screen antics of his heroes, no trace of a wrestling persona ever made its way into his daily life.

Unlike so many children today, what he watched on television stayed on television. It didn't seem to influence his behavior, but it influenced his mind as to what would come later for him, down the road. By all accounts Williams was not the kind of kid you had to worry about getting one of his classmates into a figure four leglock or hitting someone over the head with a chair.

If he hadn't been different, he probably would not have ended up as popular a student as he was. Acting like Stone Cold Steve Austin would surely have gotten him quickly expelled. When he attended Edna High School, he was so well-liked by his peers that they voted him Class Favorite three of his four years there. In his final year, in 1983, the senior class named him Mr. Cowboy, which was the Edna High School version of a homecoming king. He was at the top of high school society the same way he would someday be at the top of the WWF and the entire wider wrestling world beyond.

Steve Williams did have one fatal behavioral flaw, though. He was a bit of a class clown, doing his best to keep his peers entertained whether the teacher liked it or not. Every classroom has one of these jokesters, and in Williams's classrooms, he was always the one in the role of entertainer. He couldn't seem to stop cutting up, no matter how hard he tried.

But perhaps he didn't try so hard, knowing that it was something he had probably been born with. He's said many times that he thought he came from a family of comedians. It was that trait that led him to make the acquaintance of his high school football coach. Once, when he was acting up a little bit too much in math class, he was told that the teacher's husband, the coach, thought he should have other outlets for his energy, and had suggested the football field.

His athletic pursuits in high school were varied, but none of them involved wrestling. He got involved with track and field, where his specialty was the discus. He made a respectable showing in football, which is deep in the blood of every Texan.

His old high school football coach, Buzz Whitley, once contrasted the old hometown Williams with the new citizen-of-the-world Austin in the pages of *Rolling Stone* magazine. "He was a clean-cut kid," he said. "Great manners. I guess if I were to sum it up, totally the opposite of what he is now." His old coach doesn't care for the way Williams behaves these days in arenas and on television, because he has seen the effect that the public face of Stone Cold Steve Austin has had on the local teenagers. He doesn't care for the influence Austin is having as a role model, and in fact, kids wearing certain of Austin's more offensive T-shirts to school get sent home in the morning and are told to change into something more appropriate. So he has proven to be a somewhat controversial figure for his alma mater, and part of the heated debate over what is and is not appropriate for public discourse.

Still, as a youth Williams seemed to lead a somewhat charmed life. He wasn't always looking for trouble, as his created character does today. What difficult incidents he got into back in the old days was to be at the hands of others, as he tried to steer clear of them on his own. The small scar that he now has on his lip was from when a friend had an accident while driving with him around Texas and tried to change the radio at the same time. They ended up in a ditch, but it wasn't Williams's fault.

Cutting up in class proved to be a good thing for Williams, because the relationship with his football coach and deepening involvement in football led to a college scholarship. He attended North Texas State University, an establishment that has since changed its name to the University of North Texas. His athletic prowess earned him an education as he played football for the school team. He started off playing linebacker at first. He seemed born for the football field, and he began to come into his own as a competitor. Under Coach Corky Nelson, he played on the team for two years, honing his abilities in 1985 and 1986. By then he was a defensive tackle, and had a remarkable senior year. His statistics show him as having had fifty-five tackles, one sack, and one interception.

During the final game of his senior-year season and his college football career, his team faced Northeast Louisiana. Williams played a major part in the team's 28-20 victory. He faced down the star quarterback, Stan Humphries (who went on to his own sort of success as the San Diego Chargers Super Bowl quarterback), and the man who would eventually be the Rattlesnake had six tackles, one interception, and one sack. That final victory allowed North Texas State to finish the season with a 6-4 winning record for the year.

But all was not perfect in Williams's life. Even then, the injuries that would eventually plague his future wrestling career were mirrored in what his body was telling him. His knees were beginning to give him trouble, but he fought them with every ounce of his being and managed to stay and play in every game senior year.

It's quite clear that before entering the squared

circle, Austin had been able to find success in other arenas, such as football. It's a history that Vince McMahon would do well to keep in mind in the future. The owner of the WWF should look to him for advice on how to get his recently announced football league, the XPW, off the ground.

As a college senior, Williams looked back on his football career and felt that he wasn't good enough to go pro. He thought that he didn't have what it took to make it in the big leagues, and so made choices that led to a lot of twists and turns along the way. But we beg to differ—the sport of football could have used him.

As soon as the last game of the season was over, Williams was gone. He never graduated from college, having realized that it was not going to deliver the life he had planned, and he never felt that the rules and strictures were a good match for him anyway. And he was right. He didn't need a diploma to make him the master of his eventual profession, which is yet another way that "Stone Cold" is not the best of role models. He had to look elsewhere, and find his education in a different and very unlikely schoolroom, one with ropes, a canvas mat, and four turnbuckles.

But that didn't happen yet. First, with the scholarship money gone and a college campus seeming the wrong place for him, Williams had to look elsewhere to make his way through life. For a brief period he excelled at unloading trucks on a freight dock. That he would do well at anything he chose was an understandable attribute for someone as driven as he was, but doing well at slinging boxes wasn't what Williams had planned for himself. He had other dreams, and schemed for a better life. He knew that it was just within his reach, but he wasn't quite sure how to get it.

The dock job went so well that they even wanted to make him a supervisor. But Williams saw that as a trap. He knew that if he accepted the promotion, he might be there until the day he retired, an old man who had nothing to show for himself except calluses.

But then one day, while watching television, he saw his salvation, and it was exactly what his parents had warned him against. If that day had been a cartoon, you would have seen the proverbial lightbulb blink on over his head.

Steve Williams had found his ticket out.

chapter 3

The Bottom Line

For most of us, television commercials are a curse. We do not suffer them well. The yammering pitchmen get in the way of the programs we want to see, trying to convince us that their laundry detergents will make our clothes whiter, that their coffee will make us feel more alive, and that driving their cars will help get us there faster. And the harder they try to close the sale, the more we mistrust them.

For Steven Williams, frustrated dockworker and college dropout, a television commercial changed his life. Between long stints working, he saw a commercial on TV for the local wrestling school run by "Gentleman" Chris Adams. Austin has been asked many times about those uncertain early days, and how he got started on the path that ended him up in the wrestling ring.

"I was playing football at North Texas State University and my scholarship ran out so I paid for a semester on my own," Austin recalled. "I was working on a freight dock at the time, loading and unloading trucks, so I used to go down to the Sportatorium and watch the von Erichs wrestle there in Dallas, Texas. . . . I said, if those guys can do it, I can, too. So basically, I got into a wrestling school, and about five months later had my first match. About six years later, I ended up in the World Wrestling Federation."

Packed into one short paragraph in that way, Austin almost manages to make it seem easy. But it was to be a long, hard road ahead. Every successful wrestler who attends a school has stories of the ones who fall off along the way. Signing on for such a course doesn't guarantee anyone success. Far from it. Only the smallest percentage makes it all the way through a class, and an even more infinitesimal fraction manage to make it in the big-time. But according to all reports, Williams was a good enough physical specimen to make it with no problems, with enough determination to get him through the grueling regimen. He graduated from the Chris Adams wrestling school ready to take on the world, and began wrestling in 1989 in the South.

But Williams got more out of the school than just a shot at a new career. He also got himself a new partner in life. Eventually, Chris Adams's ex-wife, Jeanie Clark, was to marry Austin and appear by his side as a valet named Lady Blossom in both the USWA and WCW. With Jeanie, Austin was to become the father of two and stepfather of one. She has since retired from the valet business, but for a long time they were considered inseparable.

Like all beginners, Williams was cocky and sure he knew it all, but once out on the road and in the ring, he learned that it was quite a different story. Starting to take his lumps, he found that he didn't know as much about wrestling as he had thought. Suddenly, Williams didn't feel as if he had learned as much from the school as he really needed to get by. Some of the basics were his, sure, but that was about it.

He'd learned how to fall without breaking his neck, which was good, because you needed to be able to get up and do it all over again the next night, but all of the important stuff was left out. Not that it was Adams's fault, because some things can never be taught or learned in a class setting, but Williams discovered that he hadn't learned what he needed to make magic: the secret of how to make a match flow to create the best drama for an audience, or how to concoct a personality that would win over a crowd.

That sort of knowledge, he realized, would

only come in the ring in a real world match. And so it was time for school to be over, and for the real world to begin.

"There really is no formal education," he said in a radio interview with Michael Landsberg, the host of *Off the Record*, where his special appearance got the show an audience three times its usual size. As is usual, when Austin does something, it gets noticed, and so his comments on the difficulty of a wrestler getting the proper training was broadcast widely. "You don't get a degree. You might get into the ring with someone who don't know nothing, so you are compromising your health right there. Maybe some steps should be taken to get people to be a little more safer, but that's just the way it is."

That's an aspect of wrestling that hasn't changed. One thing that has is the makeup of the various federations, which probably meant more opportunities for beginners when Williams was starting out. In those early days, before Vince McMahon had crushed most of the competition and gathered them under one umbrella known as the World Wrestling Federation, there were numerous small local organizations that dotted the country, and the USWA, or United States Wrestling Association, was the one that included Williams's home state of Texas.

Fans who know "Stone Cold" Steve Austin now would not have recognized him back then as Steve Williams stepping into the ring. Even laying pictures side by side, it's difficult to believe that they're the same man. The differences are startling. Back then he was playing the hunk role rather than the tough guy persona, and with his long blond hair and tight spandex pants, he was the sort of wrestler that the Austin of today would scorn. It seemed like the thing to do at the time, but there would have to be some changes made before he got fully launched on the road to stardom.

But there's nothing wrong with that—change is what the wrestling world is made of. It's almost to be expected. Coming up with one's public face is a hit-and-miss proposition. Far more characters fail than ever succeed. Some wrestlers try on a half a dozen different personae before they find the one that clicks best with an ever-fickle audience.

The USWA sent Williams packing to Tennessee, and as is typical for the disorganized way wrestling worked back then, the local promoter there didn't have any idea that he was even arriving. But it didn't matter—they made a slot for him quickly. He was to climb into the ring there for the first time the very next day, having to improvise routines against wrestlers he'd never even met before.

Climbing out of the ring after that first bout, Williams was feeling pretty good about himself, but he was quickly forced to face an unpleasant reality for any newcomer. The promoter pulled him aside to give him a brutal assessment of his abilities.

He'd been embarrassingly terrible in the ring.

The promoter didn't care for him at all. Williams had no flair, nothing to distinguish him from other wrestlers. He was green, and the man didn't want Williams in the ring again until he could figure a few things out. At the time, fresh from battle, the news stung. He was eager for his next match, but that wasn't going to happen any time soon. He was benched, forced to sit on the sidelines to do nothing but watch the other matches and get himself a real-world education.

That hurt—until he saw the other wrestlers in action and realized that the promoter was right after all. He studied the way they made the audience respond with their words and actions. And he knew that something was missing in his presentation. Even after all his training, he was still as raw as they come. He had a long way to go.

Learning to work the audience like a pro and earn their cheers was still ahead of him. He knew that it would come eventually. But first there would have to be some changes made, and the first thing that had to go would be his given name of Steven Williams.

It wasn't something he was eager to do.

Thanks to the unhappy promoter, Tennessee was the state where Williams changed his name and reinvented himself for the first time, but history is a slippery thing, and there's more than one story as to how that changeover happened. One story has the appellation chosen by Williams, and the other has it forced uncomfortably upon him. The truth of the matter may never be known, but one thing is indisputable: While trying to turn pro and carve out a successful niche for himself, Steven Williams turned out to have a name problem. He was cursed by the fact that it was not an unusual enough name. Also, unfortunately there already *was* a Steve Williams in wrestling, and just as in the acting profession, whoever gets there first wins. The other Williams was a wrestler who grappled under the cheery nickname of Dr. Death. That Williams was well-known at the time, and was so notorious that our Williams needed to differentiate himself.

He began to look around for a new name for himself in order to avoid confusion. It had to be something quick and catchy, something that audiences could easily remember. He decided to rename himself after the title character played by Lee Majors in the 1970s television show, *The Six Million Dollar Man* because it gave off an aura of strength, toughness, and invincibility.

And so Steve Austin was born.

But that's only the way the story goes now. As with all myths, there's always more than one version. Others say that the local promoter who yanked him from the ring also ordered Williams to change his name to avoid confusion, and that Williams had no choice in the matter. As they were having their fateful discussion, a television set was blaring in the background. By chance, the TV that was on in the promoter's office was tuned to that seventies show, and he realized that a bit of borrowing might be in order. He was given the name on the spot. When Williams balked, refusing to accept the new name, he was told to try to think of a better name right then and there. He couldn't, and so the name stuck. (And it's a good thing that it did.)

As with all legends, this bit of information might be apocryphal. Wrestling fans might never know which is correct.

Once he was back in the ring as Steve Austin, things didn't get any easier, at least not immediately. It was a difficult life, one of endless travel for low pay. No one was going to get rich on what a beginning wrestler earned in the ring. The newcomers did it for the proverbial love of the game. If they weren't as tough as nails, they crashed and burned, and realized there had to be easier ways to put food on the table.

"I paid my dues," Austin once said, trying to make sense of those first few difficult years. "I got beat up. I got stitched up. I worked hurt. I starved. I did it all." But he knew that there had to be more to life than an endless cycle like that.

The only thing that kept him going was hope. If he was one of the lucky ones, he might someday trade in the tough times for the lottery ticket of a career he could cash in down the road at one of the larger organizations. But he soon learned that you can't eat hope. He was only getting twenty bucks per match. Struggling to earn that fee a half a dozen times per week wasn't an easy thing, as he'd often have to drive hundreds of miles across state lines to pick up the paycheck. What made it even harder to wrestle was an empty belly. Funds ran so low in those days that he sometimes had to live on tuna fish and potatoes. If he was lucky, and one of the scheduled matches was televised, he doubled his paycheck to forty dollars, but that still didn't keep away those times when things were tight and he was stuck eating *only* potatoes.

Austin bummed around the independents for years, wondering whether he had made the right choice. The loading dock that he'd once run from was starting to look more desirable. There's a lot to be said for a regular job with regular hours and a regular paycheck. But Steve Austin never considered himself that kind of a regular guy. He needed something more.

Some small successes started to come his way. In 1990, he won the Texas Wrestling Federation tag-team belts with fellow wrestler Rod Price. In 1991 he battled Jeff Jarrett for the Southern title and won, but the belt was taken away by referee Frank Morrell on a technicality. He was managed for a time by the infamous Paul Bearer, who now works with such superstars as the Undertaker and Kane but back then was known as Percy Pringle and was himself struggling for a piece of the spotlight.

So he wrestled, and lusted for the big-time, dreaming of being called up to either the WCW or WWF. He knew it would happen someday, which made the striving worth the wait. He kept trying to figure out a way to make himself more attractive to both audiences and the potential bookers he knew were waiting out there. After his first few months of wrestling, he decided—or once more, was told, it's difficult to know for sure which it was—to stop playing the hero and start being a villain. Or, in the parlance of the wrestling insiders, to give up on being a babyface and instead try on the part of a heel.

Austin wasn't sure that was the way to go, not when the field's biggest stars at the time were do-gooders like Hulk Hogan, who told kids not to stay up past their bedtimes. He was afraid he wouldn't be able to make it big by being bad, but by that time in Austin's career, he was willing to try anything.

It was then that the big-time beckoned, and Ted Turner's World Championship Wrestling decided to give him a shot. It seemed that all of his hard work was finally about to pay off.

But if he thought that all of his troubles were over, he would discover that yet another part of his wrestling education was still waiting for him around the corner.

chapter 4

The Hollywood Blond

Ask Steve Austin today about the World Wrestling Federation's main competitor, World Championship Wrestling, and he will surely tell you what he once he told *Sport* magazine: "I've seen their show, and to me it sucks." When interviewed during the half-time show of the Super Bowl, he even described his time in the WCW as "piss poor."

But he might have given you a different answer had you asked him a decade ago, back when he was hungry, desperate, and willing to do anything to go pro in the major leagues.

At the time, it was a thrill to move from struggling with per match fees to instead earn a regular salary. Whatever Austin says about the WCW now that he's the king of the wrestling world, back in 1991 he sure didn't mind taking their money. After a span of time subsisting on potatoes, he now had a contract in his pocket paying him $75,000 per year. He'd hit the big-time, with high school gyms having given way to packed arenas.

Austin made his WCW debut on June 3, 1991, not knowing at the time that he'd only stay with the organization for four years and that it would end badly. He wasn't yet Stone Cold—that was still half a decade away. He started out as "Stunning" Steve Austin, a pretty boy like many another striving wrestler. The fans didn't sense anything immediately special, and the powers-that-be weren't sure that they had made the right decision. The hunk persona that he was going with did not seem to fit who he really was. He was not comfortable with it, yet at the same time he was unsure exactly what personality he *would* be comfortable with.

WCW wasn't sure what to do with him. They expected big things out of Austin, and they weren't getting them. They kept pushing him to go with a gimmick of some kind, any gimmick. They didn't care for his stripped-down, no non-sense appearance, and in those glitzy times for wrestling they wanted him to deliver something more. But Austin balked. He didn't want to do that, he just wanted to be a grappler of the sort he had grown up loving. He wanted to be a wrestler, not a clown. Somehow, he got left alone for a while by the suits in an uneasy truce.

It wasn't that Austin was loath to try something new. He knew that wrestlers try on new personalities all the time, and unless they click both with who they really are and with the audience, those invented characters do not stick. He had been around the block, and knew that he just had to find the right riff. He would find it, he believed, if he took a new direction, and it would happen if he could figure out what *he* was.

It wasn't as if he wasn't having his small successes. During his first month he was even given the opportunity to dethrone the WCW TV Champion Bobby Eaton. He managed to defend and hold onto that title until April 27, 1992. So they were giving him his shots. But there didn't seem to be any buzz about him yet, and until a wrestler gets that, he's nowhere.

The fans first began to pay attention to this talented newcomer on October 27 of that year. They sat up and took notice at the Halloween Havoc pay per view, when his fifteen-minute battle with Dusty Rhodes showed that Austin had the right stuff and impressed the old-timers. Rhodes was a barroom brawler from West Texas who knew how to kick butt, low on technique but bursting with raw power, and Austin was a perfect match for him. The bout ended in a draw, but the

Rattlesnake had his chance to show his stuff, and suddenly was someone to keep an eye on.

On the surface, things seemed to be going well for Austin. He was beginning to get the attention of the fans and his peers, and during his second year with the WCW his salary was raised to $150,000. Potatoes and tuna fish were a thing of the past.

But still, the WCW was not sure quite what to do with Austin, so they put him together as a team with his friend Brian Pillman. They worked for a while as the tag team known as the Hollywood Blonds. For many years the Hollywood Blonds wrestling team was one of the hottest draws of the WCW.

"Flyin'" Brian Pillman was a former pro linebacker for Cincinnati. The six-foot, 226-pound Ohioan started grappling in the ring professionally in 1986 and joined the WCW in 1990 under the name the Loose Cannon. His motto always was, "It's not the size of the dog in the fight that matters, but the size of the fight in the dog," and his rough-and-tumble ring action showed that the man had the guts to back it up.

Austin's career-threatening injuries were nothing compared to what Pillman faced over the years. Pillman had to have his ankle fused in early 1997, and struggled to fight his way back to the ring and stay in shape afterward. Unfortunately, his quest had a tragic end, as he died from a heart attack in October 1997. Since his death, the Brian Pillman Memorial Event has been held each year to raise money for his widow Melanie and his two children: daughter Brittany and son Brian. The other wrestlers know that the life of anyone in their profession is a difficult one, and that no matter how lucky they felt, they, too, could end up in the same situation. As a result, athletes performed for free in this noble cause.

Reminiscing, Austin feels that Brian Pillman was the closest friend he ever had in the business. When Pillman still lived, they talked even when they were out of the ring, calling each at home constantly. "He was one of the smartest guys I ever knew," Austin has said, allowing himself a brief moment of sentimentality. "Not a day goes by that I honestly don't think about Brian, and I miss him." In the world of wrestling, where each man is always looking to get a leg up on his peers in the struggle to the top, such friendship is a rare thing.

The Hollywood Blonds were the most successful tag-team champions that the WCW had in 1993, and during their tenure at the top they were the premiere duo of the WCW. They represented a new age of wrestling, a younger generation coming to take over the mantle of greatness. They first won the championship from Ricky Steamboat and Shane Douglas on March 2, 1993, and their matches to defend the title were legendary.

Some of the old-timers resented the attempt to push them aside. One pair of champions who did not care for the snotty kids coming in to take over was Ric Flair—allegedly the favorite wrestler of former president George Bush—and Arn Anderson, a legendary member of the Four Horsemen. But then, Austin and Pillman made themselves easy targets for Flair, the man who was called the Nature Boy. Ric Flair was angry with the Hollywood Blonds for the way they had been sniping at him, mocking him and his long wrestling career with their "Flair for the Old" routine.

But it wasn't easy to take the title away from the Hollywood Blonds, and Flair and Anderson were not the ones to do it. Austin and Pillman held tightly onto the title for five months, until Arn Anderson took it away on August 18, 1993, with partner Paul Roma filling in for Flair. (Though the night the Blonds lost the WCW belts, Austin, too, had a substitute, in the person of Steven Regal.)

The Hollywood Blonds were very successful,

but then suddenly, inexplicably, they were broken up. Austin feels that the team was shut down not for marketing reasons or due to a loss of popularity, but purely for behind-the-scenes political reasons. While not naming names, he still holds a grudge over the split. So, for whatever reasons, the team was compelled to break up. What's more, Austin and Pillman were transformed from close friends into bitter enemies, with many dramatic fights crafted around the clash of blond versus blond.

That's where the WCW differed from the WWF, as far as Austin was concerned. In the World Wrestling Federation, business was business. Vince McMahon might have had issues with Austin's character at first—some of which were later to play out in the ring—but he was willing to let the Rattlesnake run with the character to see what would happen. No issue but the roar of the crowd should ever affect a wrestler's future. McMahon is a smart enough businessman not to let his personal feelings stand in the way of what makes good business sense. But back at the WCW, other issues were up front, and personalities were interfering with Austin's progress.

Not that it didn't make sense for Austin to break away from his partner and try to make it on his own. Even he didn't feel he had enough freedom as part of the team of the Hollywood Blonds.

"I had no room for creativity," he has said. "We were just a couple of jackasses—cocky, obnoxious smartasses." And that worked for a while, causing the audience to sit up and take notice, but it did not get Austin the *individual* attention he truly wanted. As the man's fans know today, what he does best, he does alone. And it doesn't take two to open a can of whup-ass. Still, due to his tight friendship with Brian Pillman, Austin would have been willing to stay longer with that arrangement if management had allowed it.

In fact, when Austin was once asked about the influences of others on his wrestling career, there was only one other wrestler that he was willing to admit to having had an impact, and that was his friend Brian Pillman. While he was willing to say that he respected such talents as Jake "the Snake" Roberts, Dick Murdoch, Bob Orton Jr., and Harley Race, the former Hollywood Blond, Pillman, was the only influence he listed.

But friendship has nothing to do with ratings. And in the WCW, he was even forced to have a feud with his former teacher, "Gentleman" Chris Adams. That confrontation followed the script that is designed for such encounters, and as these things go, the student beat the teacher. It's a story that always plays well with the crowd. Austin, of course, went on to outdo Adams in both fame and fortune.

The rest of Austin's tenure at the WCW was filled with incidents, but there was a sense that none of it involved any forward motion. There was action, but it seemed as if he was stuck in place as far as climbing to the top of the wrestling pile.

For a while Austin became part of the Dangerous Alliance, managed by Paul E. Dangerously, a wrestler who was to go on to be the founding force behind the ECW, known as Extreme Championship Wrestling.

Austin continued to compete hard, winning back the WCW Television title from Barry Windham in May 1992 for his second reign, which continued for four months until September 2, when he lost it back to Windham. Austin was managed for a brief period by Colonel Rob Parker, but that wasn't getting him anywhere, either. Parker was managing him when he beat Dusty Rhodes on December 27, 1993, where Austin won the WCW U.S. Title Championship. He was to hold onto it until Ricky "the Dragon" Steamboat took it away on August 24, 1994.

In September 1994, during a house show (that is, a nontelevised event, seen only by those in attendance at the arena), Austin became injured while battling against the crowd favorite, "Hacksaw" Jim Duggan. His knee caused Austin to miss a few months wrestling, giving him yet another chance to reconsider his future, weigh his options, and try to figure out what to do next to keep pushing forward toward his goal.

Those thoughts turned into action when, on May 6, 1995, Steve Austin walked out of the WCW. He'd had enough.

Austin was sick of being treated like a jobber. (This is yet another bit of insider lingo. Jobber is the name for the sort of grappler who will never get big, whose main purpose in the ring is to lose all the time to make the other wrestlers look good.) He realized that he wasn't getting anywhere and that the WCW didn't think he had enough of a gimmick to make it with the masses. Austin believed that they thought he just wasn't marketable enough, and therefore weren't going to make an effort to push him. He figured that it was pointless of him to waste any more of his sweat in WCW rings.

Eric Bischoff, the man in charge, made a personal plea and attempted to convince Austin to return. He promised that things would get better for him, if only he would come back. Austin considered the offer, and returned two days later, even more determined to make it happen and build to the next level.

But sadly, it didn't happen, and those plans all fell apart.

Just a month after his return, with his bruised knee still bothering him, Austin left the WCW for a month to wrestle throughout Asia with the New Japan Pro Wrestling Federation. For most of us mere mortals, that sort of thing would be more of a workout than we could survive, but for a wrestler of Austin's stamina, those thirty days were supposed to be a vacation, a time for recuperation. After that tour, he was meant to come back and continue the race to the top within the confines of the WCW.

But that wasn't the script that life handed him.

While in Japan, on only his third night wrestling overseas, disaster struck.

In the middle of a match, he leapt off a turnbuckle, expecting to collide with his opponent. It was the sort of simple move he had successfully performed hundreds of times, and as he flew through the air, he didn't expect it to end any differently this time. Only, to his horror, for some reason his opponent wasn't there to help complete the routine as planned, and he landed badly. He could tell even as he hit the mat that something was terribly wrong. As usual for the

Rattlesnake, though, he kept his pain to himself.

But his silence wasn't all due to Austin's intense pride. In the wrestling world, there was another reason for his secrecy: what the news would mean to his career. He didn't seek out any medical attention, and instead tried to continue through the rest of the tour despite the pain. It's something that would have brought down a lesser man.

Somehow, he was able to find the inner resources to finish his tour. The mind boggles at the thought of wrestling through such intense agony. Once back home, Austin could not put off the inevitable any longer. He visited a doctor and learned the bad news. The injury in Japan was worse than he had thought—he had torn a triceps muscle so severely that it would put him out of action.

Austin still wanted to keep this information to himself, but now there was no way. He could not avoid the medical attention he needed. He underwent extensive surgery to repair his wounded muscle and was forced to undergo rehab. At this point, Eric Bischoff, the man who had talked Austin into returning to the WCW when he'd been about to walk out of his own volition, chose to exercise the ninety day injury clause that was included at the time in all WCW contracts.

He released Austin, whose career in the WCW was finished.

To this day Austin has not forgiven the WCW for the way he was treated. His memories of the incident are still an open wound. After all the time he'd put in trying to make the WCW a success, after all the blood and sweat and energy he'd sacrificed for them, he felt that they owed him at the very least a face-to-face meeting to tell him he was canned. He had surely earned it. Instead they chose to fire him over the phone, in the way of many a cowardly boss. There he was, battered and bruised, and the news was delivered over a wire.

What bothered him most about the whole affair is that he lived at the time only thirty miles away from the WCW headquarters in the CNN Center in Atlanta. It's not as if he lived on the other side of the continent. It would have been a short drive to deliver the news in person. But they couldn't act like men, and there's nothing that Austin despises more than that.

Is it any wonder that the persona Austin eventually invented, which we all know so well, rages against such bosses?

As far as he was concerned, they had abandoned him when he needed them most. They were telling him that they had no faith in him, that they didn't believe he had a future. In the face of such an insult, his determination grew even stronger. And it had to. For with neither a pension nor health insurance, benefits wrestlers rarely see, Austin had to keep working. There was no other way.

Expecting to be at the WCW forever—and why not, as Ted Turner's organization was then at the top—Austin abruptly had to make new plans for himself. Suddenly, the WCW was out of his life, and there was no way he would beg to get back there. What Austin wanted, he took, and he never wanted to have to ask anything of anyone. So when he was finally healthy again, and once more ready to rumble, he did not return to the federation where he'd felt betrayed.

He really wanted to go over to the World Wrestling Federation, but his stubborn Texas pride prevented him from being the one to reach out and make the initial contact. He'd been busting his chops for years. The WWF surely knew who he was and had been watching his progress over the years. He felt that with the small amount of fame he already had, he shouldn't have to make the effort. It would have to be up to Vince McMahon's organization to make that first call. But the phone never rang, and so Austin had to go elsewhere for a while.

After the WCW released him in 1994, and with

the WWF failing to make the first move, Austin looked beyond the big two wrestling federations. He spent a brief period in the ECW, the Philadelphia-based group known as Extreme Championship Wrestling. While the ECW has recently come to more national prominence now that it is airing on TNN, with ever-increasing ratings, most wrestling fans at the time considered it nothing more than a farm team for the big leagues. ECW is known for its more hard-core style of wrestling, where anything can happen. Opponents are often tossed through the air to land on a bed of tacks that have been scattered in the ring, or tossed through a series of tables, or even set on fire.

Longtime wrestling fans following the trends of the field will have noticed that the WWF has been slowly starting to import this over-the-top attitude in recent years, one reason it has achieved a ratings edge over the WCW. It has even started pilfering some of the hottest ECW stars, such as the tag-team champions known as the Dudley Boyz and their heavyweight champ Taz.

In the ECW, Austin was known by the tag the "Extreme Superstar."

Because he was still injured, he only wrestled briefly in the ECW, but that didn't mean he couldn't use one of the fastest mouths in the business even as he continued to recuperate. So he was able to wreak havoc from the sidelines, and further hone his microphone skills.

His first appearance for his new employer was at the pay-per-view event Gangstas Paradise on September 16, 1995. His presence surprised them all, because he was a star of the WCW, and though he started off the appearance in the traditional manner, he soon let it be known that it was not going to be business as usual. Soon, the Austin we know and love began to come out. "I'm not going to do this shit anywhere," he complained to the commentator who was having a hard time trying to interview him. "Not even in the ECW. Because there's no way this lame-ass shit is going to get the job done, anywhere."

Austin bit the hand that was feeding him as well, believing it's what the fans ate up about his attitude. While he was in the ECW, he continually used his mouth to tell the federation that had given him a home exactly what he thought of them.

"All I've seen in ECW is a bunch of violent crap," he said on the air in October 1995, pulling no punches as he blasted the company that had taken him in. "Steve Austin is here to wrestle. It's what I do best."

At the same time, he also took shots at the

WCW, blaming them for his failure to climb to the top. "The politics in WCW," he said, "kept the biggest potential superstar in wrestling on the goddamned ground." And he was right about that unlimited potential, even as others doubted him. He just had to find a venue worthy of him.

During his brief run in the ECW, he eventually donned a black wig and began to spoof WCW executive Eric Bischoff. Playing the part, Austin called the WCW Monday broadcast "Monday Nyquil." Bischoff and the other WCW powers must have winced watching Austin take them on by saying things like, "If I don't put you to sleep, the matches probably will." He also took potshots at the WCW's biggest star, putting on a yellow and red costume and doing a mean Hulk Hogan impression, getting out more of his anger and frustration.

Finding the inner fire to pull this off was no problem for him. It was simple for Austin—no acting was required. "It was easy," he'd said. "I was angry for real. Hell, I'd just been fired."

He did not wrestle for his first three months at ECW, giving his fists (and triceps) a rest, just using his motor mouth as a weapon. Looking back at tapes of Austin then, it's easy to see how valuable this time was for him. He was becoming a master at riling a crowd, and other wrestlers as well. He was making more important gains in his skills during this fallow period than he had while wrestling almost daily.

"I was rehabbing, and I couldn't do anything but interview," he told *Texas Monthly* of this period between the WCW and the WWF. "I didn't have a character. I gave basically real-deal-style interviews, shooting the truth from the ECW platform."

Once he was back in fighting shape there, he went on to have only three matches in the ECW, against the likes of such wrestlers as the Sandman and Mikey Shipwreck, but he wasn't getting the push he wanted and felt he deserved. Austin was starting to get concerned about his career again. His ECW career did not garner him any title matches there, which he wanted desperately, causing him to worry again about the future. He knew that he could make it if only given a chance by the bosses at the top.

"Maybe Steve Austin is never going to be the superstar that everybody thought he was going to be," he said at the time in one of his few moments of doubt.

Little did he know that greater glory was still ahead, because before the doubts could grow, the World Wrestling Federation came calling.

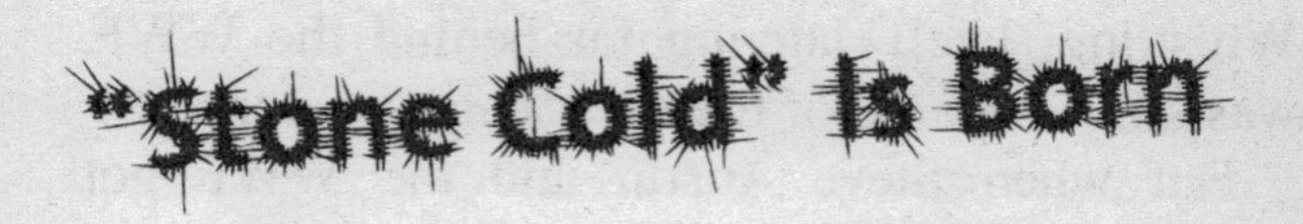

chapter 5

"Stone Cold" Is Born

In the year 2000, Vince McMahon's World Wrestling Federation rules the ratings roost. It is an unstoppable entertainment behemoth with a chokehold on the public's imagination. The audience of its many weekly programs constantly outdoes those of the competition, by a ratio of at least two- or three-to-one. Its Thursday night prime-time show *SmackDown!* even contributed to the rising fortunes of UPN. Nowadays, if you think wrestling, for many people that means WWF.

But the WWF was not the same powerhouse it is today when Steve Austin first got his call. Far from it. McMahon was fighting for his life. The federation was still reeling from the allegations of steroid use that were leveled against McMahon by the government. He was eventually acquitted of all charges. The WWF was also being beaten weekly in the ratings by an opponent with deeper pockets. Ted Turner's World Championship Wrestling, lately lagging far behind the WWF, was still in charge of the wrestling world then.

But when Steve Austin and the WWF got together, the fortunes of both began to change. Austin was at last going to be where he was meant to be.

Even then, the climb to greatness did not happen overnight.

Austin has made himself into the multimillion dollar champion, but he wouldn't be where he is today if not for the wrestler known as the Million Dollar Man, Ted DiBiase. Everybody's got to have a gimmick, as wrestling skills alone are never enough, and DiBiase's was easily understood: what he couldn't earn, he'd buy. Referees would be paid off to see things his way, and fierce enemies would be bribed into being friends.

DiBiase had been looking for years for a warrior worthy of being his Million Dollar champion, or so the storyline went. Steve Austin, needing to be reinvented for the WWF audience of the time, was perfect to fit the bill. DiBiase was made his manager in the ring.

Viewers lucky enough to catch the episode of *RAW Is WAR* that aired on December 18, 1995, saw Austin first step into the ring in the WWF. He still was not the Stone Cold Steve Austin we know today, as the powers-that-be felt the need to saddle Austin with a glitzier gimmick. He debuted under the name the Ringmaster, something that Austin never cared for but was willing to endure to get back in the thick of things. He was to be known as the Million Dollar Champion, which tied into DiBiase's own gimmick as the Million Dollar Man.

The costume Austin donned must have been painful for the simple man in black we know now, but at least he was wrestling again. He was forced to don green trunks. He wore an oversized dollar sign on his belt. DiBiase gave him the Million Dollar Belt to wear, but what was supposed to be a diamond-studded belt looked like cheap rhinestones even from the cheap seats. It was originally intended to be far worse than that, but Austin was able to prevail somewhat—at least he was able to keep them from gussying him up in the singlet they wanted.

Austin tried to pull it off with as much dignity as he could. The persona he put forward bore no relation to the sort of man he was, and he knew that the audience would sense that.

Austin was right. Wrestling fans were not immediately taken with the character. "Underwhelmed" is a good word for it. And Austin knew it.

Part of the problem is that he wasn't allowed to

be himself. His fortunes closely tied with those of the blustery DiBiase, Austin was forced to act as a sidekick instead of being his own man. And as wrestling fans have learned, Austin is no good as a sidekick to anyone.

He had to get out, and get out fast, before the same fate that befell him in the WCW came to him in the WWF. He knew what happened to wrestlers who didn't make a big impression fast: they were discarded, and he might not get another chance. Austin was determined that he wouldn't end up like one of those. Besides, there was nowhere else to go. He planned on being here, but as for what those plans fully entailed, well, he kept that to himself.

Austin knew what he wanted from day one in the WWF. He longed for a championship shot from the beginning, but though he was as boastful in the ring as any other wrestler, he kept quiet about it where it counted. He didn't want to come off as trying to grab for more than he was due, even though that was the image that eventually most suited him. He had to pay his dues in the WWF first.

But he also had to reinvent himself.

There are many pieces to the puzzle that add up to a picture of Stone Cold Steve Austin. One of the first things you notice is the lack of hair, a tough guy look that announces to the world that he just doesn't give a damn what you think.

Austin always hated having long hair when grappling in the ring, though that was the norm in wrestling in those days, and, to a great extent, even today. It made no sense to him. All it meant was that during a bout there was something else for an opponent to grab onto. He was tired of the look, tired of being just one of the boys, tired of getting hair constantly ripped out—and to be honest, tired of the fact that his hairline was receding anyway.

There's nothing wrong with a shaved head look, but balding—that was another story altogether.

One night he was watching the hard-boiled Quentin Tarrantino film *Pulp Fiction*. That film not only revolutionized modern cinema, it set the wrestling world on its ear as well, for Austin was taken by the look of Bruce Willis as an aging prizefighter with a clean-shaven skull. That image helped Willis's career, and it helped Austin's, too, for the Rattlesnake decided that was the look for him. He didn't do it all at once, though. He took it in steps to try out the look. First he got himself a crew cut, and wrestled like that for a while, but then he decided to go all the way, and shaved it all off in Pittsburgh.

But that didn't help him much. Audiences

turned on him whether he had long hair or a shiny dome. He needed to do more, take it all one step further. He knew that it wasn't enough to simply change the outside of the package—he had to go to work on the contents. No matter how hard he thought about it, no matter that he struggled as hard in his search outside the ring as he did fighting within, nothing clicked, nothing seemed right for the eternally fickle wrestling audience.

Not until a loathsome serial killer pointed the way, another example of the effects of television on Austin's life. The deadly Richard Kuklinski, known to the world as the Ice Man, was the subject of a documentary on HBO one night when Austin sat before the TV set in Georgia, and something in that special broadcast spoke to Austin. Not that he had any sympathy for killers. He just thought that a take-no-prisoners attitude like the one shown in the documentary would work in the ring. Playacting such a pissed off dude might just work at that. Austin believed that the idea of bringing into the ring someone who believed in doing unto others before they did unto him would succeed with the crowd.

So he had the basic concept. What he didn't have was a name.

Those around him were helpful. Maybe too helpful, to the point where his search became a joke. He kept trying to come up with a moniker that would carry the weight of the Ice Man, but nothing leapt to mind. The suits at the WWF thought the personality idea would work, and sent him page after page of suggestions, none of them on the mark. They didn't seem to understand what he was driving at. No one understood. Friends teased him with names that were totally off base, proving to him that no one got it.

He began to despair of finding the right tag to bring all the pieces together.

Meanwhile, Austin was tiring of being in DiBiase's shadow, a problem that soon took care of itself. A feud with Savio Vega resulted in Ted DiBiase leaving the WWF for good (he soon reappeared in the WCW). Austin was forced to fight Vega on May 16, 1996, at the Beware of Dog pay-per-view event. It was billed as a Caribbean strap match, with a condition of the bout being that if Austin lost, DiBiase would leave the federation. Austin did fail that night, and while no wrestler likes to take a fall, losing that one match might very well have been the best thing that ever happened to Steve Austin. With DiBiase gone, Austin would at last have the space and freedom to reinvent himself on his own.

Luckily, Williams's first wife, Jeanie Clark, was around at that time, because without her there would have been no such thing as "Stone Cold" Steve Austin. She was the one who spoke the phrase that sparked the idea that she decided was a perfect description of her then-husband—and so the Rattlesnake as we know him today was born.

Austin has explained many times what the couple was doing when lightning struck. "I came up with the concept behind the character," he said, "and, through a lot of frustration and a lot of trying to come up with a good name, I couldn't do it. My wife, being from England, was fixing me a cup of hot tea at the time. And I was pretty frustrated, and I told her, 'Man, I can't believe I can't come up with a name.' And she said, 'Well, go ahead and drink your tea before it gets stone cold.' She said, 'That's it. That's your name. Stone Cold Steve Austin.' That's how my name was created."

For Newton it was an apple. For "Stone Cold" Steve Austin, it was as simple as a cup of tea.

With the name finally pinned down, Austin went to Vince McMahon to discuss the entire personality package, and McMahon jumped at it. Wrestling fans could have banked that he would. That is McMahon's marketing genius. He is the Disney of destruction, always knowing the right thing to do at just the right time to feed the audience's hunger. Austin and McMahon planned it all out just a month before the annual King of the Ring pay-per-view competition. Together, they decided the way the night would proceed. That meeting between the two most important men in the business was one of the most historic nights in sports entertainment, for it helped bring us all to the realization of where we are today: that this is Austin's world, and the rest of us just live in it.

So he had the personality, and he had the name, and soon he was to have his world-famous catch-phrase, "Austin 3:16." It all came into public view at King of the Ring, which was being held that year on June 23, 1996, at the Mecca Arena in Milwaukee.

Austin had his plans for how the night would end, but it wasn't going to be an easy thing to get there. For him to earn the right to put them into action, he had to make his way to the finals. In the semifinals he fought the furious, over-the-top "Wildman" Marc Mero (now known best as the husband of Rena Mero, aka Sable). The bout with Mero got ugly quick, because Austin didn't really care about winning. If he had, he wouldn't have tried to inflict pain the way he did. Austin wanted not just to defeat Mero, but to humiliate him as well. Poor Sable wandered helplessly at ringside, unable to do anything to help her husband. Austin won swiftly, but needed eighteen stitches once the match was over—though not from anything Mero had done. It seems that Austin had bitten his own lip in the midst of the battle.

The ringside commentators were shocked that Steve Austin had gotten that far, speaking both of that night and of his brief WWF career—which shows exactly how far the man has really come. No one considers Austin in those sorts of terms any longer. No one is shocked these days at how far Austin goes. He's at the top of his game, and today the commentators know that better than anyone.

Austin's eventual opponent, the man against whom he would unveil his newest approach to wrestling, was the scripture-quoting Jake "the Snake" Roberts. Though Roberts had been wrestling for years, he had recently taken a new approach to his personal and professional lives, a more Christian approach, and often quoted the Bible in interviews. Austin decided that he would have to counter this with a bit of scripture of his own creation, and in doing so, came up with the wrestling catchphrase of the century.

In hindsight, the match itself was almost inconsequential. It was what came later that mattered most.

Roberts had injured his ribs during an earlier bout, and Austin spent most of the match battering the man where it hurt the most. This newer, nastier temperament was attractive to the fans, and Austin went at it full force.

After making the pin and watching Roberts stagger from the arena, Austin climbed to the King of the Ring throne, looked into the camera, and then, in a growl that seemed more suitable for a wild animal than a man, said, "You sit there and you thump your Bible, and you say your prayers, and it didn't get you anywhere. Talk about your psalms. Talk about John 3:16."

And then he said the eight fateful words for the first time: "Austin 3:16 says 'I just whupped your ass.'"

The interviewer seemed shocked at hearing such talk. The John 3:16 to which Austin was referring is the passage, "For God so loved the world, that he gave his only begotten Son, that whosoever believeth in him should not perish, but have everlasting life." It was a sign that was being held up in sports arenas across the country, in the hopes that the camera would catch the message on the posters and cause the viewers at home to remember who was really in charge upstairs. Now Austin was insisting that he was in charge in the ring, and he was writing his own sort of scripture. The more religious wrestling fans were not happy that Austin was making this sort of biblical reference, but there was no way to take it back. The phrase had taken on a life of its own.

Since then, Austin has uttered those words while standing over virtually every WWF wrestler around, and now the words "Austin 3:16: I just whupped your ass" are plastered across the T-shirts of wrestling fans all across the country. Austin paraphernalia is the greatest moneymaker of the WWF. Speaking of his brainstorm, Austin says that it was "just something I said and it's stuck around. It was tongue-in-cheek." He's very casual about it, but he'd better check out that cheek for some more pearls, because those words have made the merchandisers rich.

The phrase "Austin 3:16," and Austin's rugged personality, were not the only things that proved controversial about the Rattlesnake. There was another piece of the Austin puzzle that was causing controversy.

Or perhaps they should be called *two* pieces of the puzzle, because it was two middle fingers that Austin held up both within the ring and on national television. It was not a gesture that had previously been used within the ring, particularly not in the more family friendly Hulk Hogan era, and those double digits were the subject of much debate both within and without the WWF. The reasons for and against were weighed carefully.

Pundits point to them as one more sign of the coarsening of American culture. Wrestling fans point out that it was a gesture that was unlikely to have been previously unseen elsewhere by kids. And if parents didn't want to let the children see them, they could put the kids to bed early or change the channel.

"I don't expect the TV or anybody else to raise my kids," Austin has said.

But the gesture seemed to be the perfect sign language for the perpetually pissed off Stone Cold Steve Austin to let his feelings be known.

There was one other arrow to add to the Austin arsenal. What was needed was the perfect finishing move, that capper to a match, the last thing an opponent sees before being declared a loser.

Finishing moves are an all-important attention grabber for any wrestler. They are as much a part of the grappler's identity as the costume or name or rap. The best of the best know this, and don't win their fights with just any move.

Triple H has the Pedigree. The Rock uses the People's Elbow. There's always that moment in the arena when the audience knows when it is about to be delivered and cheers it on. Austin needed one all his own. The Million Dollar Dream that had been his own back when he was wrestling as the Ringmaster beside Ted DiBiase wasn't a good match anymore. Often, a wrestler will adapt an existing move to his own uses, which is what Austin did with something the old school wrestlers called the Cobra Clutch. Stone Cold Steve Austin fans will immediately recognize the move as it brings an opponent down, and these days will howl if anyone else tries to use what has now become known as the Stone Cold Stunner.

The Rattlesnake's signature move is as follows:

While standing in front of the opponent and slightly to one side, Austin reaches back around his neck (or her neck, should he be facing someone like Chyna, the Ninth Wonder of the World), and drops to the mat, dragging the other guy along. The opponent drops to his knees, and is shortly facedown on the mat. When Austin began to close his bouts by performing this move, the crowds reacted just the way he hoped, and he knew he'd discovered his finishing move.

Austin may play the part of an out-of-control, emotional guy who always goes with the gut, but the man behind the myth is more than that. It took brains to pull together all of these diverse parts to build a character who could be a champion. He had done something almost impossible, and brought into being a creation that somehow doesn't seem as if it was created at all. Instead,

Austin comes across as genuine. He needed to pull these pieces together, but he doesn't seem a corporately created patchwork quilt of ideas designed to fool us.

Austin seems real, a common man with a common touch, even though he is a multimillionaire. With his persona, he could be one of us. He doesn't need to pretend to be undead. He's not acting as if we expect him to believe that he could marry the boss's daughter. He seems like one of us, made by nature rather than craft, even though to Austin it surely must have looked as if it was taking an awfully long time for the carefully planned pieces to come together.

But at last, the pieces of the puzzle were complete—the "Stone Cold" name, the tough guy personality, the 3:16 phrase, the outstretched fingers, and the stunning finisher—and a Rattlesnake was born.

Audiences drank it up like free beer.

As he began to compete through the arenas of the world, the level of the reception he was getting surprised even Austin himself. He expected to be soundly booed, but the response was instead deafening cheers.

This shocked him. He thought that the new character he'd come up with made him a heel. With the abusive way he was acting in the ring, audiences should have wanted to see him crash and burn. They should have *enjoyed* seeing him take his licks from the good guys, but wanted him to get thrashed nonetheless. It didn't make any sense.

Others who wrestled beside him began to tell him otherwise, that he wasn't the heel he thought he was. Instead, he was a face. As he kept insisting that it couldn't be, they kept insisting otherwise. That was when Austin realized that things had changed. The clean-cut black-and-white world that he'd seen as a kid avidly watching the TV screen in Texas no longer existed. All of a sudden, instead of heels being despised and faces being loved, everything had turned inside out.

And Austin was going to take that to the bank.

"I had taken a lot of pride in being a heel," he has said. "But suddenly I realized I am a babyface. What's up with that?"

What's up with that was the biggest payday the wrestling world had yet seen.

chapter 6

King of the Ring

Stone Cold Steve Austin's multifaceted career in the World Wrestling Federation deserves not just a few short chapters in a paperback book, but instead an entire multivolume encyclopedia spanning an entire bookshelf of its own. Why is that? Not because Stone Cold said so, but because Stone Cold wrestled so.

"They don't call me the toughest son of a bitch in the World Wrestling Federation just because I need another nickname," Austin has said, and his record certainly proves it. He's won the WWF Intercontinental title twice—on August 3, 1997, and November 9, 1997—the WWF tag-team title three times—on May 25, 1997; July 14, 1997; and July 26, 1998—and the WWF World Championship four times—on March 29, 1998; June 29, 1998; March 28, 1999; and June 28, 1999.

Asked whether these accomplishments might

have come about as the result of steroid use, Austin's response at a hostile press conference was simple. "You know," he said, "whether I have or haven't, I really don't see what difference it makes."

"And probably none of your business, quite frankly," tossed in Vince McMahon.

Austin's career in the WWF has been marked by an intensity that never wavers. That is why the fans love him. They know that he gives his all for them.

"As soon as I became WWF champion for the first time, I swore to myself that being on top was the only place for me," he has said. "There ain't no damn need to put on my black trunks and my black boots if I'm not the best. Being second-best is a waste of my time."

His career highlights support this.

He fights to win. And even if he loses, it is very rarely cleanly. When he falls, some behind-the-scenes political machinations are usually the cause. For example, he lost the 1999 Royal Rumble to Vince McMahon only when he was distracted by the Rock. On *RAW Is WAR* in February 1999, though he was pinned by Vince McMahon at the finish of a corporate gauntlet match, he had to go through Ken Shamrock, Test, Kane, and Chyna to do so.

McMahon didn't defeat him on the up and up. It took the Big Bossman knocking him down with a whack of his nightstick to cause him to lose to McMahon.

It got worse. In May 1999, Austin lost the world title to the Undertaker at the WWF Main Event thanks to Guest Referee Shane McMahon, the boss's son, who might be considered a bit biased in terms of defending all things corporate. Shane made a fast count, and even Vince had to get involved in the melee that came after.

At King of the Ring, Austin had Shane and Vince decimated at a handicap ladder match, but could not reach the suitcase hung over the ring because a backstage enemy kept raising it out of his reach. Within that suitcase were the papers that would give corporate control of the WWF to whomever got to it first in a Handicap Winner-Take-All Ladder Match for control of the WWF. It was a gruesome battle, as whoever climbed the ladder was tossed off it.

"You can go up the ladder," Austin threatened. "You can go down the ladder, you can go around the damn ladder—you can rest assured that both your asses belong to Stone Cold Steve Austin."

But the match was over when, with Vince and Austin battling atop the ladder, Shane tipped it over, knocking both men to the mat, so that he could then climb the ladder and grab the suitcase, ending Austin's plans.

That may be part of Austin's unending popularity. The WWF storylines may get manipulated to cause Austin to lose the title, but when he does, we're always allowed to continue to think of him as being victimized by those richer and more powerful than him. It's a conspiracy of the haves against the have-nots, and Austin is always there representing the rest of us.

So it didn't matter whether he won or lost—audiences loved him anyway. It was his persona they admired, not his win-loss record.

Over the years, Austin has faced some of the fiercest competitors the WWF has created. Perhaps the most ominous was the Undertaker, aka Mark Calloway, a six-nine, 328-pound destroyer who began wrestling under such names as Texas Red, the Master of Pain, and the Punisher. When he got to the WCW in 1990, he fought as "Mean" Mark Callous. He didn't get to the WWF until 1991, where he invented the Undertaker, the lord of the undead.

The Undertaker has been one of Austin's main rivals. Austin lost the title to him on May 23, 1999, but won it back only a month later. Austin has used the "Stone Cold" Stunner on the tattooed giant many times. He defeated the Undertaker at a Buried Alive match at Rock Bottom to qualify for the Royal Rumble.

Austin didn't mince words when talking about the Undertaker in the pages of *Wrestling Yearbook:* "The Undertaker is nothing more than a damn stooge who decided to take the easy way out by hooking up with McMahon. Until he can beat 'Stone Cold' like a man, one-on-one, I ain't got no damn respect for the dead man."

Paul Wight, aka the Big Show, has been another feuder with the Rattlesnake. The Big Show came into the WWF on February 14, 1999, aligned with the McMahons to help them get Austin. (When he first appeared, he was known as the Big Nasty.) He eventually got a title shot against Austin, and the Rattlesnake managed to hold onto his belt by slamming a metal folding chair repeatedly against the giant's legs. Wight defended himself the only way he knew how—with a vicious choke-slam that not only propelled Austin to the mat but *through* the mat. Austin went down through the canvas onto the floor of the arena, which made the big man feel good at first, but the move cost Wight the title, as he was disqualified.

Wight later changed his tune about Austin, however, going from enemy to ally.

"I saw him on TV and read about him in the

magazines, but I never really got to know him until after I got out of the corporation," he said, explaining his transition at the time to the press. "He's top shelf. When McMahon offered me a job in the WWF, he poisoned my mind about Austin, and of course I believed everything he said. He was paying me big bucks to hate Austin. Stone Cold and I have talked, and I assured him that I'll do everything in my power to help him bring McMahon and his whole damn corporation down."

Austin has even had his run-ins with the female contingent of wrestling. On February 25, 1998, in front of 16,110 fans at the In Your House pay-per-view event, Austin was part of an eight-man tag-team match, which he won by pinning "Road Dogg" Jesse James. At the fight's end, Chyna, the woman who has been dubbed the Ninth Wonder of the World, objected to his triumph and entered the ring. She pushed him, but gentleman that he is, Austin tried to shrug it off and leave. But Chyna wouldn't let him ignore her. She grabbed and turned him, and gave him the upraised middle fingers that Austin feels he owns. He wouldn't take this from anyone, not even a woman, and gave her the Stone Cold Stunner.

"She's one tough bitch," Austin has said of the only woman ever allowed to enter the Royal Rumble—a woman, by the way, whom he chose to eliminate from that competition himself. "I'm not the kind to forgive and forget," Austin has said, and he certainly showed it at the Rumble.

Austin knew when he first got into the WWF that in order to get big, he had to choose big targets. As soon as he heard that Bret Hart was going to be jumping ship to return to the WCW, he began deriding Hart and everything he stood for every opportunity he got. He knew there would be a big buzz once Hart returned, and he wanted some of that to rub off on him. His plan worked, because once the rumors turned into reality, it was announced that Hart would face him at the 1996 Survivor Series to seek revenge for all the insults. They would go on to have one of the greatest WrestleMania matches of all time.

But his biggest target, the one that would be perhaps the greatest feud in wrestling, was with the boss himself, Vince McMahon. Most corporate owners stay in the background, but McMahon is in the mold of New York Yankees owner George Steinbrenner, whose antics are often part of the allure. Though not the allure for all of us. Phil Mushnick, writing of McMahon's planned new football league in *TV Guide*, wrote that "McMahon makes John Rocker look like Ghandi." (And speaking of *TV Guide*, Vince McMahon was reportedly livid when Steve

Austin appeared on the cover of that magazine, apparently believing that the honor should have been his. *TV Guide*, however, was happy with the choice—the 1999 cover with Austin was one of the bestselling issues of the year.)

Even as the readers of *Wrestling All Stars* ranked Stone Cold Steve Austin as the most popular wrestling figure, they said that the man they most hated was Vince McMahon. The difference between Mushnick and wrestling fans, however, is they *like* not liking the WWF boss.

McMahon is the man who made small-time wrestling into big business. High school gymnasiums are a thing of the past. In 1987, for example, at the Pontiac Silverdome in Michigan, WrestleMania III set an indoor event attendance record of 93,173 that has still not been broken.

McMahon has been masterminding the WWF for decades, but it was Austin who finally forced him to wrestle. It brought McMahon new fame in addition to his wealth. But perhaps it was better that he didn't, for he reportedly still has nightmares from the Stone Cold Stunner he received at Austin's hands at WrestleMania XV.

Offstage, in the real world, McMahon is effusive in the praise he gives the Rattlesnake. He told *Cigar Aficionado* magazine: "What people like Steve Austin do with their bodies—combining

Sue Schneider

J. E. Sports Photos

Austin at the Emmys and in the ring

J. E. Sports Photos

Time for a Steel Cage match

Celebrating with a Steve-weiser

J. E. Sports Photos

Albert L. Ortega

Don't mess with this man!

Michael Lano

Austin smiles with hard-core wrestling hero Dory Funk.

Michael Lano

Austin with first wife and valet "Lady Blossom"

Michael Lano

Jeannie keeps her eye on the belt.

Michael Lano

Do you recognize this longhaired blond?

Michael Lano

Austin takes his lumps!

Stone Cold climbs the ropes.

J. E. Sports Photos

The fans love him!

Albert L. Ortega

The happy couple: Debra and Stone Cold

athleticism with performance—is nothing short of incredible."

And Austin has similarly praised McMahon. He's called the head of the WWF "pretty damn close to being a genius. Do I like him? Do we see eye-to-eye? No. But I give credit where credit is due."

But is that the way their relationship has played out within the arenas of the world? Far from it.

Will any of that mutual admiration society credit ever be given onstage where the fans can see it? Not very likely.

In front of the microphones, McMahon rants on with statements such as: "The only thing worse than Stone Cold being World Wrestling Federation champion is Stone Cold being the CEO." And Austin volleys back with: "Stone Cold Steve Austin is having a blast running your stupid little company."

The boss makes a show of hating the unruly employee. Says Pat Patterson in *The Wrestler*, "Every time Vince sees Austin in that ring with the belt, drinking beer and doing everything else he does, his blood starts to boil. That's how much he hates Austin. . . . I personally think this feud might go on for years and years."

Austin knows this, and that makes the gold all the more cherished. "McMahon would probably rather have this belt strapped around the waist of some wino that he just pulled off the street than have me holding onto it," he said.

Of such hatred economic miracles are made.

Austin has been the poster boy for rebellious employees. After putting him in the hospital, he has attacked McMahon with a hospital bedpan. He's even threatened to shoot McMahon with what turned out to be a toy gun, an incident that was perhaps too frighteningly real.

McMahon turned his hatred of Austin into one of the more elaborate ruses in wrestling history. A conglomeration of wrestlers known as the Corporate Ministry, ruled by a masked man called the Greater Power, endangered McMahon's own daughter, but at the end it was revealed that the Greater Power was McMahon himself. So great was his hatred of Austin that McMahon was willing to let it ruin his whole family.

"I used to think that [McMahon] had sunk as low as a human being could ever sink," said Austin of the debacle, "but to then make believe you're on one side when you're on the other, and to risk your daughter in the process? Hell, that's the lowest I ever heard. Let me tell you something—he's dead meat, 'cause Stone Cold said so."

But messing with family is a bad idea, because

wrestling—at least in the WWF—is a family affair. In response to this discovery about her husband's role in her daughter's abduction, Linda McMahon, CEO of the WWF, resigned her position and turned the reins of power over to Austin, whose response to this sudden influx of power was predictable. He announced that there would be no more business as usual. There would be no more corporate control. Workers no longer found the need to congregate around the water cooler, as Austin began supplying them with his traditional brewskis. He fired a member of the board of directors and hired one of the mail clerks in that person's place.

"Linda asked me to do it," Austin told reporters later, "because she knew, and so did I, that Vince's beady little eyes would practically pop out of his damn head when he found out I had every right to walk around WWF headquarters and have people start doing things my way."

Then came the King of the Ring ladder match, where Austin lost control. It was just as well. Austin was never suited to the corporate role. He belongs on the outside, rattling the bars of the corporate cage so those inside stay nervous.

"I'd much rather get in there and bust the Undertaker's head wide open and get paid for it than sit around an office all day."

One of the most dramatic encounters was when Austin defeated Vince McMahon at St. Valentine's Day Massacre in Memphis to earn the World Title Match at WrestleMania XV. He fought him in a steel cage match, in which the first contestant to break out of the cage and get free is declared the winner.

McMahon took a tough beating. He was beaten with the very hospital gurney that was meant to take him from the field of battle. He was slammed through the Spanish broadcasting table and choked with electrical cord. McMahon was even handicapped by his own blood running through his eyes. And when Austin was finally ready to leave the bloody pulp of a boss behind him, McMahon goaded him on by giving him the finger, drawing back the Rattlesnake, perhaps angered by Vince's use of his own signal. Paul Wight moved over from the WCW to make his WWF debut at this event as the Big Show, breaking up through the mat into the cage, interfering by trying to help Vince. Instead, Wight caused Austin to win by destroying the cage and letting Austin out, which gave the Rattlesnake the shot at the reigning champ the following month.

"Hell, I know how much that son of a bitch hates my damn guts. Being the stupid jackass that he is, he just keeps raising the stakes against me."

And nowhere were those stakes raised higher than at the Royal Rumble.

The 1999 Royal Rumble, usually a circus to begin with, turned into a "Get Austin" crusade on July 24, 1999, at the Arrowhead Pond Arena in Anaheim, California. McMahon placed a $100,000 bounty on Austin's head. Whichever of the other twenty-nine wrestlers eliminated Austin would win the prize.

It was to be the ultimate showdown between Austin and McMahon. If there was any doubt that this sport entertainment was scripted, you need only look at who drew the first two numbers of the night. Austin was the first man to enter the ring, which meant that he would have to survive against twenty-nine other men, each coming in at ninety-second intervals. McMahon made sure that he was the second man in, which was the most dramatic way the night could have gone.

Even though McMahon set the situation up, he didn't want to face what he had created. He quickly escaped from the ring—not being eliminated, as one must be evicted by another wrestler, not by one's own choice—and was chased throughout the arena by Austin, the battle extending through the balcony, and even into the women's rest room. But a trap was set for Austin there, and he was beaten unconscious by other members of the corporation and taken to the hospital.

McMahon was happy. Not only did he get rid of Austin, but he didn't have to cough up the $100,000 as a reward. As the Royal Rumble continued, McMahon watched with joy and even did color commentary from ringside as the Rumble proceeded. But that joy ended when Austin returned to the arena in a commandeered ambulance.

He reentered the ring, rather than going for McMahon, extending Vince's agony. At one point, with McMahon rooting for his paid assassins, Austin even came down to toss a pitcher of water in the boss's face, then returned to the ring to continue cleaning up the riffraff. But he eventually ran out of opponents and was able to turn his sights back to the boss. When Vince pleaded with the Rattlesnake, Austin's response was to slam him with a headset. He chased McMahon into the ring and inflicted great punishment on him. But he went on for far longer than was needed to win the match, which was Austin's mistake.

The Rock came running down the ring and took Austin's mind off the business at hand. As the winner of the Rumble was guaranteed a title shot at the next WrestleMania, the Rock wanted the chance to beat Austin right then. While Austin was distracted, the unthinkable happened. McMahon made his move and emerged victorious.

Austin eliminated more opponents from the match than any other contender: Golga, Ken Shamrock, Billy Gunn, Test, Chyna, Triple H, Owen Hart, D-Lo Brown, and the Big Bossman. But he could not eliminate his most hated enemy, Vince McMahon—who tossed Austin out of the ring when he wasn't looking—to become the winner.

But it wasn't enough for McMahon to merely win—he had to mock Austin as well. He rubbed the defeat in his face, climbing the turnbuckle and gulping down a brewski.

The next night on Monday night *RAW*, McMahon offered to mold Austin into the proper corporate champion. When asked whether he wanted to see Austin rise to the top, McMahon said that only if Austin changed and became respectful, which as we all know would be impossible for the Rattlesnake. McMahon said that Austin as champion would be "a public relations corporate nightmare."

But Austin would have none of it. "You ain't gonna mold me," he said. "You ain't gonna break me. What you see, Vince, is what you get." Angry that he'd had the match stolen from him the previous night, Austin delivered a solid Stunner on

McMahon, and the boss had him arrested for assault, something that would happen far more frequently if the antics within the ring were treated seriously. Austin figured that after all that McMahon had done to him, why shouldn't he?

"They've screwed me over more times than I can count," he said. "Why shouldn't I do everything I can to screw them? The only problem is, I'm having one hell of a good time doing what I'm doing."

Once, to play with McMahon's mind, Austin did give himself a corporate makeover, which lasted one night. He came in wearing a suit, and allowed McMahon to feel for a moment that he had succeeded in bending Austin to his will, which would make his defeat all the sweeter to Austin. Then Austin ripped off the fancy duds to reveal his black shorts and T-shirt, and to assure the world that Steve Austin would never change.

But the fans need not have worried. Austin could never kowtow to anyone, not even if he wanted to.

"I spent the better part of this past year fighting an S.O.B. by the name of Vince McMahon," said Austin, looking back on the events of 1999 in the pages of the *Pro Wrestling Illustrated Holiday Special*. "I've been screwed over and over again. I spilled buckets of blood to get where I am today.

The bottom line is that I'm a vindicated man. I'm standing on top of the mountain while Vince McMahon has been driven out of the WWF with his little tail between his legs. And that's all I got to say about that."

McMahon has been out of sight in the WWF while Austin has been recuperating from his injuries, but you can rest assured that as soon as Austin is ready to return to the ring, McMahon will be right there in the role of fiendish boss.

The all-time greatest feud in professional wrestling is far from over.

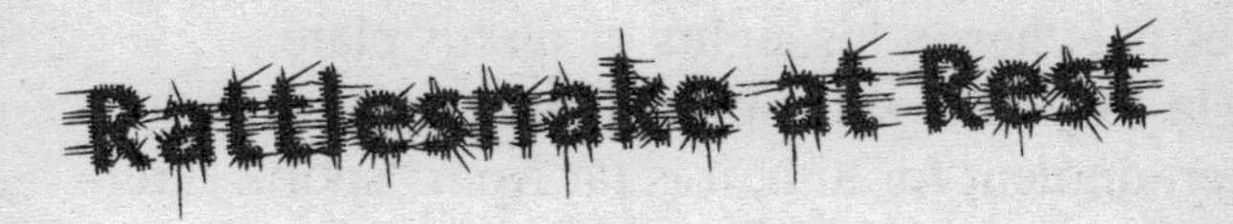

chapter 7

Rattlesnake at Rest

Stone Cold Steve Austin has a well-known reputation for being a loner, so it is understandable that his pursuits outside of the ring are usually those he can enjoy for the most part on his own time and on his own terms—though he does occasionally let a few of his special friends join in the hell-raising fun.

His pleasures are simple and few, and one of them, at least, is far from politically correct in these times that are tending away from the red-blooded and toward the vegetarian.

Unlike Goldberg, the shaven-headed champion of World Championship Wrestling, who has been taken up as a poster boy by animal lovers since he has made the better treatment of the furry and four-footed his personal cause, Austin is no defender of the animals. Far from it. Austin is a nightmare for the members of People for the Ethical Treatment of Animals. He believes that the only proper place for most woodland creatures is either in his sights or on his plate.

He loves the sport of the hunt, and while it is entertainment for him, it is far from "sports entertainment" for his prey. What he loves to hunt most are deer, his favorite targets. Friends who have tried to convince Austin to spend his time going duck hunting instead have discovered that to be a losing proposition. He owns over twenty guns, and when he uses them, he wants to turn them on something he considers worth eating, and scrawny birds just aren't on his list. And he's such a good shot that his opponents in the ring are lucky that the deadliest weapon he uses there is usually a steel chair. Austin rarely misses. If you got to his house, you might see the work of his taxidermist, with whom he hunts and drinks regularly.

When he's not hunting, he likes to cruise the highways, riding around in a truck with the window wide open so he can feel the wind on his face, letting his mind wander as he thinks toward his next bout and the next foe he has to demolish. Bumper-to-bumper city traffic is not for him, because Austin is usually looking for speed. Whether or not he drives fifty-five he won't say, but we suspect that the Rattlesnake has been known to put the pedal to the metal once in a while.

When not controlling tons of metal, Austin is a man who knows how to enjoy his beers. To him, they are more than just props he uses in the ring to celebrate yet another victory. He knows how to savor them like fine wine. When he talks about tossing one back, he jokingly calls them Steve-weisers, but the beer that he means when he says it, what he really likes to drink, is Coors Light. You wouldn't think that Austin would go for a light beer, but even though he gets quite a work-out every time he steps into the ring, he has to keep far away from the high calorie stuff. It turns out that wrestlers, surprisingly, have to be as calorie conscious as supermodels.

"I got to watch the gut," he has said.

When it comes to music, Austin prefers to listen to either country or heavy metal—but that's about it. There's no rap music for this son of Texas. He wouldn't let it come out of his speaker or into his ears. He has said that if you were to take a ride with him, the radio in his truck would be tuned to country 85 percent of the time.

Austin has been known to play pranks on other wrestlers, and he gets a big kick out of them. One of the more publishable ones was reported by Mick Foley, known as Mankind and Cactus Jack. It seems that once upon a time, between matches, Austin and Mick Foley went to the beach. They both got in the water and then, while Foley was distracted by the beauty of the sun and the sand, Austin vanished. Seeing his friend gone, Foley decided to do some girl watching, and began to look around for some babes in bikinis. But he was puzzled, because wherever he looked, all he could see were men holding hands, gazing deeply into each other's eyes, and kissing.

Austin had abandoned him on a gay beach.

Many of the pastimes attributed to Austin seem right in keeping with his "Stone Cold" character. But there is one that seems contradictory for him. Surprisingly, one of the things he likes to do is collect antiques. It is difficult to picture this hulking giant in such a situation as anything but a bull in a china shop, yet that is what Austin professes. Maybe it's because older furniture is harder for him to break.

More a personality trait than a hobby is the fact that Austin, for all his bravado, is a little superstitious. There are certain things he must do the same way all the time, or else he fears that life will go against him. For example, when he gets ready for a match, he always puts his right boot on first, and when he tapes up his wrists prior to getting into the ring, it is always the left wrist first. That much about him is unchangeable. He isn't even sure why he does this, but that's the way life is—it just feels right.

Truth be told, Austin can't afford to do much out of the ring, so blistering is the pace of his career. His livelihood *is* his life, and everything else has to remain secondary. He barely has time for other pursuits. He makes no secret of this. In an interview on MTV, Austin has indicated that what he most likes to do is "to stay home and relax and try to heal up."

Yet only a person like Austin would call even his out-of-ring regimen relaxing. Regardless of what else is going on in his life, he works out every day, wherever he happens to find himself. His exercise routine would probably crush a lesser athlete, but for Austin it is somehow reinvigorating.

Some wrestlers have earned reputations for growling at the public when approached between matches, having an attitude that shows they've forgotten who brought them their fame, but when found outside the ring, Austin is very good to his fans, something not lost on his peers, such as fellow grappler Edge. "You see a guy like Steve Austin," he has said, "who is always busy, and anytime a fan approaches him, he's always cool with them. When you see one of the top guys being that accommodating, it trickles down to everyone else." Hard to believe, but it turns out that Austin can be a good role model after all!

There is one time, however, when fans are most definitely unwelcome, and that's when Austin is communing with a brewski. Sure, he'll be glad to chat with you in a bar, but if you come up behind him while he's seated there, remember one very important fact: don't dare lean over his shoulders or put your hands on him when he isn't looking. He hates that. His ring instincts are on radar alert, and he couldn't be blamed if he suddenly used them on you.

But what he likes best, what refreshes him the most—more than a cold brew, a monster truck, and a deer in his sights—is, plain and simple, going to work. He's a working man at heart, but you'll never hear him singing the working man's blues. There's nothing out of the ring for Austin that is as good as what he gets inside the ring. His worst day in the squared circle is better than his best day on the streets.

When his theme music plays and the crowd starts to roar, it's a high that no sideline hobby could replace. His two favorite moments in life are when he enters the ring to the blare of guitar riffs pounding and the sound of glass breaking, and when he gives the Stunner.

And nothing makes wrestling fans happier than that.

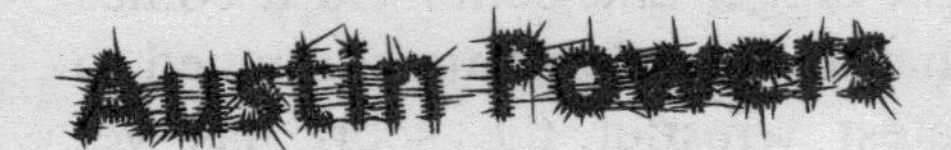

chapter 8

WrestleMania has always been known as the place where giants walked the Earth. From the start, it was intended to be the Super Bowl of the newly defined world of sports entertainment, and it succeeded in delivering what its boastful claim promised. Vince McMahon invented it beginning March 31, 1985, at Madison Square Garden, the nation's premier arena in the heart of the Big Apple. WrestleMania was to be a place and moment in time where the best and the brightest competed.

It changed the history of the sport.

Mainstream stars such as Liberace, Billy Martin, and Muhammad Ali were given guest-starring roles on that night, and the rock and roll connection—which was to bring wrestling to new heights—began as well, because songstress Cyndi Lauper was there to help revitalize the sport. Over one million people paid to watch on closed-circuit TV. The annual WrestleManias that followed only got bigger and better. So it comes as no surprise that as WrestleMania continued to thrive, the greatest wrestler the sport has yet known has given stellar performances time and again at these, the greatest events in wrestling history.

Austin was to start out as a winner from the very beginning of his participation at these prestigious events. In his very first appearance, which was WrestleMania XII in 1996, he was forced to face the fiery Savio Vega, putting his Million Dollar Belt on the line. At the Arrowhead Pond in Anaheim, the popularity of wrestling caused a new attendance record of 18,852 to be set for the locale.

The foes of Vega and Austin went into their match with some ugly history behind them. The fans were ready to see the outcome of a long, drawn-out feud. The two men had been forced to be tag-team partners the previous week, and it had not gone well. Whenever Vega called for the tag, seeking help from the Rattlesnake, he was ignored. Austin would not tag in. Austin was not interested in winning the tag-team titles for them. He couldn't care less about the belts at that moment, just about causing Vega pain, so he did everything he could to sabotage the title event.

So there was plenty of bad blood, enough to power a main event, but to show how Austin was regarded back in 1996, this match was scheduled for early in the night, a sign that his fame had not yet come and that Vince McMahon did not yet have confidence in his drawing power. It was early in Austin's career yet. These days, now that he is the top dog, the match he's in is held for the end of the night, regardless of who he's fighting, to keep the audience living in anticipation. But back then, that most important of spots was held for Bret Hart and Shawn Michaels and their grueling Iron Man Championship. Still, the audience was primed and looking forward to seeing Austin and Vega settle their differences.

One of the strangest aspects of this night from our vantage point of a new century, where Austin is the king of wrestling, is that the Rattlesnake got no mike time. He fought with his fists and didn't get an opportunity to use one of his most dangerous weapons—his mouth. All of the prefight chatter went to Vega, who was a volcano of threats. How things have changed, now that the world has grown used to Austin controlling a crowd's emotions with his words. Fans today would never allow Austin to remain silent.

Austin entered with Ted DiBiase, the self-styled Million Dollar Man, who was still Austin's manager at the time, and who had given Austin the glittering Million Dollar Belt. It was draped over one of the Rattlesnake's shoulders, as if Austin dared anyone to try to take it away. Just from the expression on his face alone, most men would have thought it impossible and not even bothered to try. But Savio Vega was not like most men, and on top of that, he was angry.

The audience got what they had come for, as both men quickly began to whale away at each other. They seemed evenly matched at the beginning of the match. They attacked each other furiously, and were slugging as if in a barroom brawl. It was a triumph of strength and anger over technique, and no one could tell how it might end. The slugging soon turned to head butting, and the two men seemed to fight as equals, with neither having an advantage over the other. The fight continued out of the ring, where it seems all fights must go at least once per bout, and Austin was the first to be knocked to his knees by the power of a blow.

The match was fast and furious, with many covers, far more than normal. Back and forth they went, alternating the upper hand between them, with one Vega cover so close to the three count that it almost seemed he had Austin pinned.

In addition to the placement of the bout in the night's agenda, there was further proof that Austin was not yet considered a big enough star to keep the attention of the audience, at least as far as Vince McMahon was concerned. The match was interrupted many times—quite bizarrely—by McMahon and Lawler giving updates from ringside on the aftermath of Roddy Piper's previous back-lot brawl with Golddust earlier in the evening. The camera cut away so that Piper was shown in a white Ford Bronco chasing the fleeing Golddust, using footage that had been lifted from the infamous O. J. Simpson chase.

Austin fans watching a replay of this match today will surely be thinking, "Knock it off!" Having Austin play second banana to Piper and Golddust would be unthinkable today. Three times the viewers were shown this sort of footage instead of the action in the ring, and looking back, we can smile, because we know that soon the world would learn that the same mistake should not be made.

Another unusual aspect of the night for fans who only know Austin from his most recent years is that there was as yet no animosity between the Rattlesnake and the boss, for McMahon and Lawler described the match calmly, taking no sides between Austin and Vega. If McMahon were in the same arena today with Austin, he would be unable to resist frothing at the mouth and railing at the Rattlesnake. But back in 1996, McMahon considered him to be just another wrestler.

The tide changed late in the fight when Austin made a leap from the top rope in an attempt to pin the fallen Vega, and instead discovered, to his dismay, that Vega was still conscious enough to lift a foot that slammed into his face. With Austin downed from that blow, he used expressions we have not seen him use for years, and gestures he would never dream of utilizing today. Austin shook his head from side to side and waved a hand toward Vega as if to ward his opponent off, a tactic more often used by such as Ric Flair than by the man we have come to know as "Stone Cold," who would neither give mercy nor expect to receive it.

With Vega suddenly in charge, the battle proceeded so furiously that the referee was knocked out and unable to declare a winner. DiBiase, who had been doing little more than cheering his man on, and whose strategy was knocked for a loop because he was used to bribing officials as part of his act to get his way, used the absence of a ref's watchful eye to hand the Million Dollar Belt into the ring. As the challenger was distracted by DiBiase, Austin slammed Vega with the metal of the belt. When Vega went down from the blow, Austin slammed him with the belt yet again.

Austin was now back in charge, and ready to be declared the winner, but with the ref still out, there was no official to award him the title. Austin put his then-signature move sleeper hold, the Million Dollar Dream, on Vega. (That move is another aspect of Austin that has gone the way of DiBiase, off to the WCW.) DiBiase tried to waken the ref, grabbing a soda from a fan and spilling it on the official's head. Finally the ref was awake again, and Austin was awarded the title.

Not bad for a freshman appearance at WrestleMania. But the following year, Austin's match would garner even more intense interest from fans and pros alike.

In 1997, Austin was to fight Bret Hart at WrestleMania XIII, facing off for the Heavyweight Championship belt in Chicago, the Million Dollar Belt being a thing of the past.

Bret Hart is part of a wrestling dynasty. He was trained in the famous Dungeon by his father Stu Hart, who has also been responsible for getting an amazing number of today's finest—such as Chris Jericho, Rowdy Roddy Piper, and Chris Benoit—ready for the ring. Hart's tagline of "the best there is, the best there was, and the best there ever will be" is one of the most famous boasts in wrestling, and Austin couldn't resist trying to prove him wrong.

Neither man was at his best going into this match. Hart (who has since moved on to the WCW, and whose long career was the focus of the award-winning A&E documentary *Wrestling with Shadows*) had not worked in six months due to injuries. Austin, no stranger to injury himself, went in wearing knee braces.

Hart hated Austin. Coming from the old school as he did, and believing in the traditional face of wrestling, he saw Austin as destroying everything that was good about the sport. The man who believed only in the excellence of execution saw Austin as representing the death of heroes. He wanted the ring to be a noble place, an arena with no room in it for beer-swilling, cursing, middle-finger-waving lowlifes.

As for Austin, he was already a two-time Intercontinental Champion, but it was time for something more. It was time to climb to the next level, to where he wanted to be all along. It was time to show that Hart's famed tagline was just a lie.

Neither man wanted to just win the match. They each wanted more than just the championship belt.

They each wanted to destroy the other.

The rules of the bout seemed designed for just that. Rather than using just one of the ordinary referees, a special referee was assigned—Ken Shamrock, billed as the world's most dangerous man, a fine wrestler in his own right. And it wasn't slated to be a standard pin match. The encounter was to be a submission match. One wrestler couldn't conquer the other by merely pinning him for a three count, which would be difficult enough. This rule meant that the only way the match would end would be for someone to quit. And uttering those words of resignation is something Austin would never do. Neither the man nor the character he'd created had ever done such a thing.

This bout was considered by most students of the squared circle to be one of the most brutal matches in the history of wrestling competition. It figures that Austin would be a vital part of it.

Such was the power of these men that the fight could not be contained within the ropes, but instead ranged all over the arena, allowing the fans to get up close and personal with their heroes. One wonders how the poor guy selling sodas and trying to meet his sales quotas felt when Austin grabbed for his tray and dumped all of his drinks over Hart's head.

Bret Hart kept trying to put his finishing move, the Sharpshooter, on Austin. When Austin proved too slippery for him, Hart used a metal folding chair to attack Austin's vulnerable leg. Hart kept working on Austin's knees, hoping the pain of the old injuries would flare up.

The ugliest part of the match occurred when Hart slammed Austin headfirst into the steel steps, which meant that Austin spent much of the match bleeding profusely from his head. It was something rarely seen in professional wrestling in either the WWF or WCW—there is violence aplenty, but somehow it always stays below the level of a bloodbath. But the night of WrestleMania XIII, brutality reigned.

Austin could barely see to defend himself, but still he refused to submit. Hart knew that the wound he had opened on Austin's head would be the key to his triumph, and so he kept working on it. Covered with blood, forehead lacerated, Austin looked in sad shape, but his spirit was still strong. Whenever Shamrock looked to see whether Austin was ready to submit, the Rattlesnake answered in defiance with his two upraised fingers.

Austin made a few feeble efforts to win, such as his attempts to choke Hart with microphone wires, but he was growing weak from blood loss, and Hart slammed Austin yet again in the face with the timer's bell. At last, Hart was able to manipulate Austin into the Sharpshooter, and time stopped in the arena.

Austin struggled to reach for the ropes, which would have caused Shamrock to have to separate the men. But it was not to be. This clash of the titans might still be going on now if Austin, weak from the loss of blood, had not collapsed into unconsciousness. Ken Shamrock was forced to stop the fight, allowing Hart to be declared the winner.

Austin, of course, did not take his loss easily. When he regained consciousness, with Hart out of his reach, he delivered a Stunner on one of the ring officials. He staggered out of the arena, waving off all offers of help. Austin had lost, but in losing, had still managed to grab himself a pivotal place in wrestling history.

After all that mayhem, Austin once more showed his toughness with the very words he was to use to describe that night. "A tough day at the office for Steve Austin," was all he would say, choosing to retain his tough guy image and keep his emotions to himself.

Austin would have his revenge, but that's another story entirely.

In 1998, Stone Cold Steve Austin was due to face off against Shawn Michaels at WrestleMania XIV. But Michaels, known also as HBK, or the Heartbreak Kid, was not the only draw for the night. Also in the arena was Mike Tyson, the boxing world's heavyweight champion, who was to play a vital role as a special enforcer, and who had been woven into wrestling's subplots for many months leading up to that night.

We first saw Tyson enter the wrestling world on January 18, 1998, at the eleventh annual Royal Rumble that was held that night in San Jose, California, in front of 18,542 fans. Mike Tyson was there in a special box seat, and whenever the camera panned toward him, he could be seen having the time of his life. Austin was to win that night, which meant that the Rattlesnake would be going to WrestleMania with a shot at the title. From Tyson's enthusiasm, it seems that Austin had a fan on his side. But it was all to go awry the next day in Fresno at Monday night *RAW*.

Blame Vince McMahon for that. He brought Tyson into the ring, and then proceeded to call Iron Mike "the baddest man on the planet," an introduction that inflamed Austin. McMahon had to have known it would, since that's the sort of title the Rattlesnake prides himself on keeping for himself. It was a deliberate challenge. To tell the boxer invading the wrestling world who was really the top dog, Austin used a bit of sign language and gave Tyson the finger. Tyson responded by pushing Austin away, and suddenly there was a brawl in the center of the ring.

Talking about it later, Austin explained how ridiculous he thought it all was. He thought the brouhaha proved again how much tougher he was than Iron Mike. Footage of that night proves Austin right, because there he was, being held down by a mob, while there was no one holding Tyson down—Tyson could have continued to fight him if he'd really wanted. The incident was in the papers all over, and not just in the wrestling press. The same way that Cyndi Lauper had done before him, Tyson had awakened the press instincts of the more mainstream media. Austin felt that he'd had no choice but to challenge Tyson after what McMahon had said. "When you step foot into the WWF ring," Austin said, "you're stepping foot in my office."

It was a long and rocky road to WrestleMania XIV. Along the way, after four other wrestlers teamed up and brought Austin down, Shawn Michaels humiliated him by rubbing the championship belt in his face and telling Austin it was something he could never have. Michaels should have thought better about gloating that day, however, because one thing's for sure—when you tell Austin he can't have something, he goes for it all the more.

Things sped up after the press conference that McMahon held on February 5, 1998, at which the bout between Michaels and Austin was announced, and Tyson, no longer impartial, was chosen as the special enforcer. On March 2, Tyson was shown to be a member of DeGeneration X, and wore the gang's shirt. Austin ended up kicked to the mat by Michaels that night. It got even worse on March 26, at a public workout being held in Boston. Austin showed up and was attacked by Shawn Michaels, Mike Tyson, and Triple H. They tied him in the ropes, and kept him there while the Heartbreak Kid and Iron Mike kissed him on the face as a further sign of public humiliation.

But Austin kept his cool. All he had to say of that day was that "Mike Tyson's a hell of a boxer, but he can't kiss worth a damn." He planned to save his fury for inside the ring itself.

The crowd's appetite for destruction was whetted by a fifteen-person tag-team rumble at the Fleet Center in Boston, but what they were really waiting for was the match between Austin and Michaels.

The first to enter the arena was Mike Tyson, wearing a D-X T-shirt and making the D-X hand slashing gestures. His loyalties were apparent, and it was uncertain whether Austin could get a fair fight under these circumstances. Austin, the challenger, came next, and it was clear that the audience was on his side. The crowd went wild as he mounted the turnbuckles and raised his hands.

Within the ring, Tyson and Austin went nose-to-nose, their animosity evident on their faces. Their words could not be picked up over the microphones, but it was obvious that each was daring the other to start something, and it looked for a while as if the big card that night might be between Austin and Tyson, with Michaels left out in the cold, the title match forgotten. But somehow, Austin's sanity took hold. He knew that he couldn't knock out the special enforcer without losing the shot at the title, and after all his years of climbing through the wrestling ranks, Austin wasn't going to throw that away, no matter how much he wanted to show Tyson who was boss. Austin pulled away as Michaels's theme music began to play.

Austin, ever the loner, had come into the arena by himself, but Michaels, at the time the most decorated WWF champion, obviously felt the need for support, because he entered with Triple H and Chyna, fellow members of DeGeneration X. Michaels was then at the top of the WWF, but even with eyes shut, from the sound alone one could tell that the champion did not have the crowd with him.

Once the bell rang and the fight started, Austin

quickly became disgusted with events. The two are different breeds of wrestler, using two different techniques. Michaels moved quickly, bounding about the ring, behaving much as Ali did when he ruled boxing. Austin was a slugger, a lumberer, an unstoppable object, and expected to go head-to-head with an opponent. He obviously didn't think Michaels's dancing was wrestling by any stretch of the imagination, and gave him the famous Austin fingers, telling him to get started with the real thing.

Michaels's response to the direct challenge was to run out of and around the ring until chased by Austin back inside the ropes. As the battle continued, Austin knocked Michaels out of the ring on top of Triple H. When Austin went out after his opponent, HHH chose to interfere, attacking Austin, but for once the officials seemed to take notice of such an event, and barred Chyna and HHH from the arena. They were ordered away, much to the dismay of Shawn Michaels. He had lost his insurance, and the fight continued without them, throughout the arena, over barriers, into Dumpsters.

Each man went with his strength—Michaels leaping and turning, Austin slugging and slamming. Michaels's back, which had caused him trouble in other matches, was bothering him throughout, and he looked pained, but the contestants managed to be on equal footing until Michaels mocked Stone Cold by giving him a taste of his own upraised fingers, which sent Austin wild. For a while Austin was on top, until Michaels put him into a sleeper hold. In the struggle to break free, Austin knocked Michaels back, slamming him into the ref, who was knocked unconscious.

The championship bout had to go on with no officiating save from Mike Tyson, who had shown himself to be no friend to Steve Austin.

The battle continued for many desperate minutes, until Michaels failed to connect with a kick and Austin was able to duck beneath and deliver his Stunner. The question then was, would there be a count-out, since Tyson was apparently against him. But then, Mike Tyson, as controversial a boxer as Austin is as a wrestler, became the ref who made the three count that gave the Rattlesnake the title. Tyson had double-crossed D-X. It was a ruse, and Iron Mike had really been on Austin's side all along!

The championship finally belonged to Stone Cold Steve Austin, thanks to another heavyweight champion.

When Austin mounted the turnbuckles, belt in hand, it was the culmination of all he had worked a lifetime to achieve. The Austin era had begun!

Shawn Michaels, recovering from that final blow, was upset to see this sorry turn of events, and took a punch at Tyson, so Tyson returned the favor. Only he did not miss, and Michaels ended his championship bout flat on his back on the mat, an Austin 3:16 T-shirt over his face. The strange months-long public animosity between Tyson and Austin had been a front to finally give Austin what he'd been seeking for years.

But that doesn't mean that Austin feels he owed Tyson any favors. Austin has said, "I want to wrestle him or box him," proclaiming his desire to tussle with Tyson, whatever the circumstances. And the way things are going for the Lone Star champion, we should all place our bets on the Rattlesnake.

Austin walked away with a belt that night, but all Michaels got was pain. During the match, Michaels reinjured two disks in his back, and was sidelined afterward. He was named commissioner in November, so even though he could not wrestle, he was able to continue to use his awesome mike skills. He went on to play a further part in the Steve Austin soap opera when Vince McMahon declared that Michaels had total control of the WWF *except* when it came to Austin.

Michaels later said of Austin, "I wish I was still

wrestling, because if I were, Steve Austin and I would be headlining every major card in the world. There would be nothing like Austin vs. Michaels, the two greatest wrestlers of the decade." We suspect that Michaels might be overstating his own importance vis-à-vis Stone Cold, but the sentiments are welcome, a sign that Austin had arrived.

In 1999, Steve Austin was once again the straw that stirred the drink. He was to fight for the world title against the Rock at WrestleMania XV. The Rock had gotten to the top by defeating Mankind in a ladder match in Birmingham, Alabama, on February 15, 1999. (The Rock had a little bit of help at that event from Paul Wight, aka the Big Show, but in the wrestling world, these things usually don't get noticed.)

As usual, Vince McMahon managed to begin on a classy note. On March 28, at the First Union Center in Philadelphia, the National Anthem was sung by the harmonizing Boyz II Men in front of 20,276 fans, bringing a sense of dignity to the occasion. But the rest of the night was not so classy.

First, in order to derail Austin's run at the title, Vince had appointed himself the special guest referee. McMahon did not want a beer-guzzling champion again, and figured he could stop the onslaught of the Rattlesnake. But just when McMahon got to the ring, commissioner Shawn Michaels, who had played such a large part in the previous WrestleMania, showed up to rain on the boss's parade, pointing out that only one man could appoint a WrestleMania official that night, and that man was the Heartbreak Kid himself. So it was back to regular officials, and McMahon would have to find another way to sabotage the event.

The Rock entered the arena carrying over his shoulder the belt that Austin had won before, and that he wanted back. But the Rock wasn't going to let it go easily, and began talking trash before the fight began. As Austin tried to play to the crowd from the turnbuckles, as he usually does upon his entrance, the Rock was in his face, forcing the match to an early beginning.

The Rock maintained an early advantage, knocking Austin out of ring and kicking him while he was down. It seemed it would continue in that way, but Austin quickly returned the favor, and took the battle out into the crowd, where Austin appeared to find strength. In fact, Austin thinks of himself as one of the crowd, and so many of his fights occur out there, where he rampages through the audience, he and his opponent slamming against cameras and choking each other with wires. It seems, then, as if the people who spent the money on the best seats in the house suddenly don't have such good seats any longer, while the folks stuck in the cheap seats in the back have the best view. Maybe that's what Austin wanted all along, to bring the show to the people who he felt were most like him.

When Austin and the Rock finally got back to ringside, they couldn't seem to get back into the ring. The Rock took a drink of water from the announcer's table and spit it in Austin's face, which Austin repaid by slamming the Rock into the announcer's table, destroying it for the night. (Luckily, this match was to be the finale.) The pair didn't get back into the ring until Austin then had a chance to take a long drink of water himself, and he spit it into the Rock's face, returning the favor done to him.

Since Vince had declared the match to be a no-D-Q match, meaning no disqualifications, chairs were legal, and the wrestlers did not have to worry about sneaking them past the refs. The Rock used those chairs well, going to town on Austin's knees without letup. But they weren't enough to defeat Austin. The blows only seemed to make him stronger.

It was an historic night not only because of the epic battle between Austin and the Rock, but also because three referees were knocked out in the course of the fight.

Austin knocked out the first referee when a chair meant for the Rock collided with the official instead.

The Rock, angry at the next ref for a slow count that stopped him from taking the title, did his famous Rock Bottom finishing move, and a third ref had to enter.

Vince McMahon, in an attempt to stop Austin from winning, knocked out the third ref himself, then joined in with the Rock by beating up on Austin, kicking and punching him. It looked bad for Austin.

But staggering up the aisle came Mankind, whom everyone had thought was in the hospital due to his earlier match that night with the Big Show. Mankind kicked McMahon out of the ring, and now that WrestleMania had run out of refs, he would be the ref himself.

The fight ended quickly then, now that things were on an equal footing and with no more interference. The Rock tried to use the People's Elbow, but Austin managed to clear the mat, with the result that the Rock slammed into the canvas, allowing Austin to deliver a Stone Cold Stunner.

Austin's win was counted off by bestselling author Mankind, letting the Rattlesnake become the first WWF star to transform himself into a World Champion three times within the same year. With McMahon distraught at ringside, Austin popped two celebratory beers.

McMahon couldn't bear the sight of it and yelled at Austin to relinquish the belt. Vince was silenced when Austin slugged him, and then dragged his body into the ring to give him a Stone Cold Stunner as well. Austin said farewell to the night by emptying a beer across McMahon's body.

This 1999 pay-per-view event was seen by 875,000 households at $34.95 apiece, earning $30 million for the WWF. Where once boxing ruled the PPV roost, now it had a new rival, for the Mike Tyson title bout with Francois Botha raked in the same amount. This match was the biggest money-drawing professional wrestling match in pay-per-view history. The thought of Austin taking back the title was just too good to miss.

Fans cannot picture a WrestleMania event without Austin, but the Rattlesnake's body might not cooperate. The recuperation time from Austin's back operation is such that there is little likelihood he will be able to appear at WrestleMania XVI in the year 2000 as anything more than a referee, an announcer, or some sort of spoiler. If nothing else, it's expected that he will likely play a part in preventing Triple H from winning the WF heavyweight title.

But when 2001 comes around, watch out for WrestleMania XVII. It will spell Austin's wrestling return to that prestigious event, and should top these first four appearances.

Maybe Austin 3:16 should really mean, "I just returned to WrestleMania!"

chapter 9

Austin Has Balls

Stone Cold Steve Austin is the king of the world of sports entertainment, but at the same time, the Rattlesnake is a fan of the more traditional sports as well. Austin has been to baseball games so many times that they should start fitting him for a uniform. The man almost needs his own locker!

How times have changed for the denizens of wrestling arenas! Once, the athletes in "legitimate" sports (if they even deserve that modifier) would not want to be seen with wrestlers, but now instead they're jealous of them, and they hunger for the same popularity as wrestlers. So it's no wonder that Austin has been welcomed with open arms in baseball stadiums across the country.

On July 9, 1999, Steve Austin was in Pennsylvania to wrestle at a live event at the First Union Center. Like all superstars, what he did for relaxation during his time off made going to the movies—like the rest of us—seem tame by comparison.

Austin took himself out to the ball game for batting practice at Philadelphia's Veterans Stadium with the Philadelphia Phillies just before their game against the Baltimore Orioles. After warming up, he then took to the plate against Terry Francona, the Phillies manager.

Fans lucky enough to have arrived in time to view the scene were amazed by the ability of the wrestler, particularly considering that players of some other popular sports, such as basketball's Michael Jordan, have not translated their skills all that well to the diamond. Watching Austin knock the skin off the ball—now *that's* sports entertainment. The Rattlesnake batted for half an hour, and after doing so without batting gloves, Stone Cold realized that he'd been swinging so powerfully that his hands were bleeding.

Afterward, the iron man of wrestling met in the locker room with the iron man of baseball, the Orioles' Cal Ripken, Jr. Which one had the better advice on how to tough it out over the long haul we can only imagine.

The next day, July 10, 1999, Austin threw out the first pitch at a sold-out game between the Mets and the Yankees at Shea Stadium as a guest of the Mets. He had previously thrown out a first pitch in May in Kansas City, but this time he showed up with bandaged hands, thanks to the workout the day before.

Before that, he took batting practice there as well, wearing a Mets jersey that had been tailor-made with the Austin 3:16 logo on it. Mets General Manager Steve Phillips said, "We're glad to have him here in case a brawl breaks out. He's in a Mets uniform, so we can run him out there to throw some Yankees around. There are a lot of times in the clubhouse the players have wrestling on, and I know he's one of their favorites." Then Austin went back to the clubhouse and hung around with baseball superstar Mike Piazza.

When it was time for the first pitch, the ovation from the crowd was overwhelming. Austin threw the pitch to Piazza, a strike that whizzed waist-high. Austin raised his arms to a rumbling roar.

"Guys are excited to meet him," pitcher John Franco said. "They want to see how big he is in person and open up a can of whup-ass on him."

Though he was there siding with the Mets, many of the Yankees came over to meet him as well.

"This is the Mets and the Yankees—this is a big deal," Austin said in the pages of *WWF* magazine. "It's always fun. One of these days I'll look back and say, 'What all have I done?' Not a whole lot of people get the chance to go out and throw the first ball out for the Yankees and Mets, and I get to say I did that."

On the mound, the crowd's roar when he raised his arms above his head was just like in the arena in front of wrestling fans. His popularity survived even outside the ring. "It was a hell of a response, and that always makes you feel good."

The odds are on Austin's side. All three teams that he's visited won their events that day, which means that if baseball has any sense, other teams should soon be giving the Rattlesnake a call real soon now.

One of the other sports Austin has gotten involved with is the racing business. His name and trademark smoking skull now appear on a "funny car" driven by veteran racer Jerry Toliver. Austin's buggy made its public debut on February 3, 1999, in Pomona, California, at the Winternationals. Austin's glaring face is emblazoned on the hood, many times larger than life.

The National Hot Rod Association is getting a taste of the whup-ass that Austin has been delivering in the World Wrestling Federation all along. The souped-up Pontiac Firebird has over 6,000 horsepower and takes less than five seconds to achieve speeds of over 300 miles per hour. With Austin in attendance watching the day's preparations at the Mopar Parts Nationals, Toliver even broke a personal record by qualifying for the number-two slot with a speed of 303.57 miles per hour in 4.96 seconds. Forget the transmission fluid—it must be the Steve-weisers.

As for other sports, Austin has made one comment regarding basketball, revealed from the days when another sports figure was invading his wrestling turf. When Dennis Rodman was making the move to wrestling, Austin was asked whether he would consider facing him in a match.

"No, I wouldn't want to wrestle him," Austin said, making a small joke, "but I would consider dating him." He added, "I might consider shooting baskets with him or something like that. But he's not in my league."

Looking at the vast panorama of wrestling personalities, it's clear that very few are.

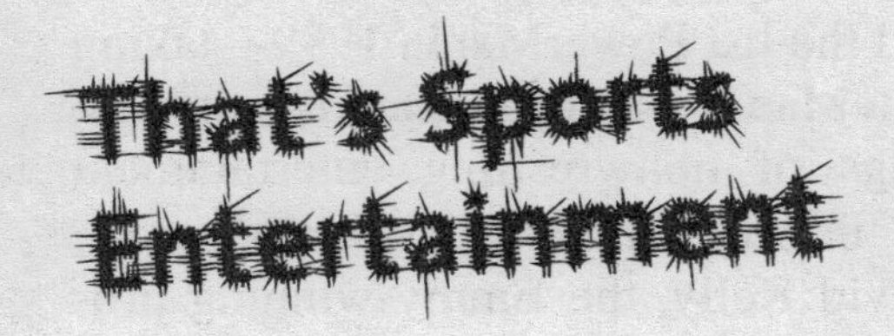

chapter 10

That's Sports Entertainment

With televised wrestling events growing in leaps and bounds, it's no surprise that the rest of television has taken a liking to this most famous of grapplers. After all, it only makes sense. Take a look at what wrestling did to UPN. The first Thursday night *SmackDown!* aired on April 29, 1999; WWF gave the fledgling network two hours of prime time that earned a 5.8 rating. *SmackDown!* is now UPN's highest rated show.

Wrestling has had an impact on the very way we look at entertainment, and Austin, of course, has been a part of that.

The annual Power Issue of *Entertainment Weekly*, in which the editors rate the one hundred most powerful people in entertainment, is always one of that magazine's most popular issues of the year. In 1999 they decided to take a look at their world with a wrestling point of view, in recognition of the influence that sport is now having. Instead of playing it straight, the editors called the list PowerMania 1999—taking off on WrestleMania—and illustrated the article with drawings of nonwrestling entertainment personalities in wrestling poses. For example, luminary David Kelly, the Emmy-winning producer of both *Ally McBeal* and *The Practice*, was portrayed in black tights.

No wrestlers come in within the top one hundred, but the WWF itself comes in—grudgingly—at 100.5 on the century list. However, guess who gets the big push in the inset illustrations for this? Vince McMahon is almost hidden behind Austin, and the caption stating that "wrestlers like 'Stone Cold' Steve Austin help give McMahon's WWF the Midas touch" show who the real world thinks is really in charge of the federation's fortunes. It isn't the man behind the throne. It's Stone Cold. And whose picture appears on the cover along with other top stars such as Tom Hanks and John Travolta? Not power broker Vince McMahon—Austin stands alone.

But Austin's ring feats aren't the only thing garnering attention. His dramatic abilities are also getting considerable notice. Austin first made a splash with a guest spot on *Nash Bridges*, the tongue-in-cheek detective drama that stars Don Johnson, Cheech Marin, and Yasmin Bleeth.

When Austin appears as cop Jake Cage, Neilsen sits up and takes notice. CBS scored big ratings with these episodes so far—his first appearance being the show's highest rated episode—and Austin quickly became a favorite of viewers.

Austin's appearances on *Nash Bridges* were different from any other appearance of a wrestler on a network television program—no wrestler has ever had a recurring role before, yet another wrestling record broken by the Rattlesnake. Also, he isn't there to be seen as a joke, but as a legitimate contributor to the advancement of the series' plots.

The show liked to play off Austin's reputed rough edges, one episode even resulting in him being given etiquette lessons so he could blend in at a fancy San Francisco wedding. Another aspect of his character shows him hooked on the Weather Channel. He even takes foxtrot lessons to impress the character Yasmin Bleeth portrays.

"Deep down, you know I'm just a pussycat," he murmured to Yasmin Bleeth. She didn't know whether to believe him, but the audience did.

His dialogue wasn't the greatest. Maybe the writers didn't think it had to be. The shouts of "Hell, yeah!" that are heard on air are a direct copy of his in-ring chatter. But no matter. When Austin shouted, "Let's go kick some ass, man!"

wrestling fans—and the show's regular viewers—did, and the ratings soared.

"What's to say?" said series star Don Johnson of Austin. "He's great. He's awesome. He's 'Stone Cold' Steve Austin."

The injuries that were bad for Austin's wrestling career and required some fancy dancing on the part of Vince McMahon and his writers were good for his acting career, for after the August 22 SummerSlam pay per view, Austin suddenly had the time for the less physically demanding filming. He was able to film five episodes while recuperating.

Austin told *Inside Wrestling* that "acting can be a hell of a lot of fun. I'd like to do more of it." Whether he will is still to be determined. There are rumors that the creators of *Nash Bridges* might spin off Austin with a pilot of his own, but a lot depends on whether his wrestling career will be able to return in full swing after his recuperation.

Steve Austin is now seen by the world as such a superhero that Chaos! Comics published a four issue miniseries about the grappler that premiered in September 1999. They'd previously started with the Undertaker, and then followed that up with Mankind. One wonders why it took them so long to get around to the number-one draw in wrestling.

Titled *Stone Cold Steve Austin: Tougher than the Rest*, the 32-page, full-color comic book was meant to mold Austin (at least according to the initial press release) as a "modern, classic Western hero, coming into town and setting things right." Combining his trademarked hard-boiled persona with elements of his *Nash Bridges* character, he was meant to be the Lone Ranger for a new generation. Watch out, Superman!

The stories were written by veteran comic book scripter Steven Grant and illustrated by James Fry, who managed to capture Austin's gruff exterior on every page. The colorful tale conveys the best of his persona. He is a loner, coming into a corrupt town to free it from the tight grip of gangs.

In the story, as usual, Austin is positioned as a common man's hero, one who does what he does with no need of training or superpowers, simply because that's the kind of guy he is. When faced with a gang attempting to use karate moves to force him into taking a position he despises, the comic book Austin proclaims:

"Think you're so all-fired tough with your cute little Bruce Lee moves. That ain't fightin'. That's dancing."

In order to increase the collectibility of this product, it was produced with several different covers, to hook Austin fans into coming back for more.

But don't think that Austin's fictional success is only two-dimensional. Stone Cold Steve Austin's strangest entrance into the entertainment world was not as a muscleman, but as an animated lump of clay.

MTV's popular series *Celebrity Deathmatch* has captured the imagination of a new generation by allowing celebrities to take part in the kinds of knock-down-drag-out fights that are usually only participated in by the grapplers of the WWF. The series was created and directed by Eric Fogel, who allied himself with a horde of clay animators. The violence is ridiculously bloody, with spines ripped out and bodies ripped in half. Some of the face-offs that have been scheduled include the Rolling Stone's Mick Jagger versus Aerosmith's Steven Tyler for a fight to the death to determine who has the biggest lips in rock and roll, and David Letterman versus Jay Leno in an Electrified Razor-Wire Cage of Death.

Of course, a fight isn't a fight unless Austin is involved, and so his likeness has been formed out of clay so he could make an animated appearance. He was so tickled by the idea that he even provided his own voice for the clay figure. When he was introduced, Austin was called a man "with a doctorate in destruction." And rather than a pay per view, the event was billed as a "clay per view."

What other odd roles Austin will take are surely beyond our imagination. But the number of times he has been chosen to make an appearance at some of entertainment's most popular events shows how closely he has been embraced by Hollywood. Though his injuries were keeping him from wrestling much, in 1999 he appeared both at the MTV Music Video Awards and the Emmy Awards.

Austin appeared onstage September 9 at the 1999 Music Video Awards to introduce the performance of rapper Jay-Z. Twelve million people watched, the most in the show's sixteen year history, and a 37 percent increase over the previous year, which leads us to wonder if the record-breaking ratings were only a coincidence, or whether Austin's popularity has in some way rubbed off. While attending the event, Austin stayed at the elegant Rigah Royal Hotel with girlfriend and grappling peer Debra. Before the ceremony began, Austin gave several interviews on the red carpet outside the Metropolitan Opera House.

Why did the Rattlesnake think fans should enjoy the rapper?

Austin explained that simply with his familiar

line, saying they should because "Stone Cold said so."

Road Dogg Jesse James and X-Pac were visible in the audience, but did not get chosen to participate in any onstage antics, a sign of how far Austin had risen above the pack. However, *Rolling Stone* magazine wasn't impressed by the Rattlesnake. In their February 17, 2000, issue they referred to our favorite wrestler as "Stone Cold Steve Austin, whose musical IQ hovers around 3.16."

We think they're just jealous. Austin has had his own success in the music business. Two different CDs have come out with his growling face plastered on their covers. First came *Stone Cold Metal*, with Austin's favorite heavy metal hits. This was so successful that it was followed up with *Stone Cold Country*, with a selection of the Rattlesnake's favorite country hits, including songs from Willie Nelson, Merle Haggard, Waylon Jennings, Hank Williams Jr., and others.

Austin is invading every aspect of entertainment.

You can't turn on the television these days without spotting him in one capacity or another. On September 12, 1999, Austin made an onstage appearance at the 51st Annual Primetime Emmy Awards at the Shrine Auditorium in Los Angeles.

He has appeared as a guest on such shows as *Live with Regis and Kathy Lee*, *Late Night with Conan O'Brien* (on August 20, 1999), and *The Late, Late Show with Craig Kilborn*. He's become one of the more popular guests on the Howard Stern radio show.

Austin even appeared in a commercial for 1-800-COLLECT, shown chucking D'Lo Brown out of the ring.

Pretty soon, if Stone Cold continues these pursuits, Austin 3:16 will start to mean, "I just won an Emmy!"

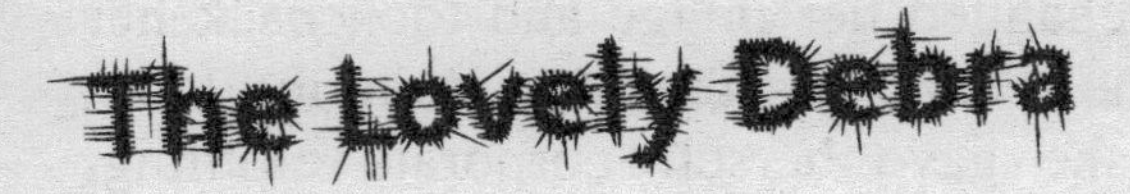

chapter 11

The Lovely Debra

Every Romeo needs his Juliet, and for Stone Cold Steve Austin that Juliet is a blond, blue-eyed beauty named Debra. It takes someone who understands the wrestling business to understand the bizarre life of a top wrestler, and so Austin is in luck, for Debra has had an active role in the WWF in recent years.

Debra McMichaels didn't begin her career in the WWF, but back in the WCW, and she wasn't using her own name at that time. She was known as the Beauty Queen, and her gimmick was that she'd come into the ring garbed in a long gown and with a tiara atop her head. She was at times allied with Ric Flair, the loudest mouth in the WCW. Eventually, she began to manage Jeff Jarrett, who billed himself as a great country singer, and who usually won his matches by bashing his opponents over the head with a guitar.

When WWF started looking more like the

place to be, Jarrett and McMichaels jumped, and she changed her image and took back her own name. Gone was the Miss America look. Instead she gave herself corporate clothing, though the cleavage that peeked through her well-tailored suits existed in boardrooms only in men's fantasies. And she had no problems with using that cleavage to her advantage whenever possible. It was her secret weapon—or perhaps it should be said that *they* were her secret weapons—and she continually used them on behalf of her partners. Whenever times got tough for Jarrett or his tag-team partner Owen Hart, Debra would give the opponents a glimpse of what lay under her shirt, and the tide would change in favor of her men.

Whenever she walked toward the squared circle, Jerry Lawler would cry out from ringside in his shrill voice, "Puppies! Puppies! Show me the puppies!" and McMichaels was never shy. She would always oblige, though within the limits of cable television's Standards and Practices departments.

In fact, she became so well known for these attributes that she appeared on the cover of *WWF Raw* magazine wearing nothing but two *literal* puppies which she held in front of her naked chest. Their tiny furry bodies barely covered

Debra, and the issue became quite controversial, even to the point of being removed from some grocery stores.

That wasn't the only controversy to which Debra's name was attached.

She was also involved in one of the more controversial events in recent wrestling history, when Sable claimed that she only lost her title to Debra because she refused to have her gown torn off on national television. Whatever the reason, fans were pleased when Debra became the WWF woman's champion by winning an evening gown match.

Her in-ring relationship with Jarrett began to crumble once he had the Intercontinental belt. Owning that trophy affected his ego, and he seemed to resent her comments about being a wrestler herself. At that point his new valet, Miss Kitty, came along, which eventually forced a breakup of Jarrett and Debra. Once Jarrett went to the WCW and left Debra behind, she had new worlds to conquer. One of them was Stone Cold Steve Austin, who happened to have divorced his first wife in May 1999. Debra McMichaels and Steve Austin are now one of the premiere power couples in the wrestling world.

In an odd turn of events, when Debra was allied with Jeff Jarrett, he generated a lot of attention to himself when he began badmouthing Austin's famous 3:16 phrase, calling it blasphemous. It did get him noticed, but not always in the way he wished. In fact, it slowed down his own career, because his public outbursts resulted in Austin refusing to battle Jarrett at the July 26, 1999, taping of *RAW Is WAR*, a match that would have brought needed attention to Jarrett's career.

Austin's stated claim was that Jarrett wasn't a big enough star to face him. Austin knows, as do most wrestlers, that you are only as big as your enemies, and so he decided to pass on Jarrett, and battled the Undertaker that night instead. But insiders feel that the real reason for Austin's hesitation wasn't Jarrett's heat, or lack thereof, but instead his anger over the fact that Jarrett's comments might slam Austin's T-shirt sales.

Not long afterward, Debra and Austin started dating. These facts of Austin's life are a perfect example of how intertwined the relationships in wrestling can be.

In the past, Debra has generally been more popular with the fans than any wrestler with whom she is attached. And the men in her life haven't always appreciated that. Life with Austin, if the offstage relationship comes alive in the ring, will change that, since he's the one hogging the spotlight. It will be interesting to see how she handles that change in the dynamic, if and when it comes.

Debra McMichaels enjoys her interactions with the audience. Fans who meet her are always surprised by how welcoming she is when she's off the camera and out of the ring. That openness can be attributed to a bad experience she once had with actress Morgan Fairchild. Debra had been a big fan of the actress, but once, when they shared a flight and she finally got a chance to meet Fairchild, Debra felt that the woman was stuck-up, too interested in playing the role of one who is rich and famous.

"You don't forget things like that," Debra said of the incident. "That totally turned me off as a fan of hers."

As a result, Debra tries harder to please in public situations, though she's discovered it isn't always easy. Some of her fans have very odd requests. She was once asked to autograph the stomach of a Chihuahua!

Perhaps that's one reason that Debra and Stone Cold have made such a good couple. *The Globe* has reported Austin as saying that "Deb's a dream gal. She's a down-home Southern gal who's become my best friend. I love wrestling, but nothing makes me happier than for the two of us to climb into my truck and drive off into the country and get away from it all."

As long as they don't get *too* far away from it all. Wrestling fans want them both back in the ring as soon as possible.

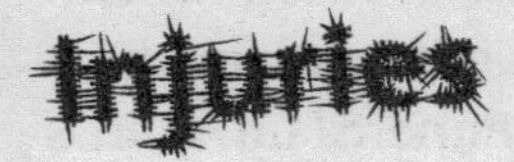

chapter 12

Injuries

Injuries are an unavoidable part of the game in wrestling. Newcomers to the sport just have to learn how to handle them, because there's no way to get around them. Over Stone Cold Steve Austin's long and illustrious career, he has been no stranger to them. His need to rely on members of the medical profession has become legendary. His injuries have been as big a factor on the arc of his career as Vince McMahon. They got him tossed out of the WCW, and they've punctuated his career with the WWF.

Perhaps the worst of them, and certainly the one that replays most often in Austin's mind, occurred on August 3, 1997, when the Rattlesnake was facing Owen Hart for the Intercontinental belt during the semifinals of SummerSlam 97. (Hart's own wrestling injury several years later was so severe that he actually died while making an entrance from the rafters during a match—falling fifty feet to his death at the Kemper Arena in Kansas City on May 23, 1999. The incident focused worldwide attention on the risks that wrestlers must take for their profession.) At SummerSlam, Hart's poorly executed pile driver—a move during which one wrestler holds another upside down against his body and then falls to his knees, giving the appearance of dropping his opponent headfirst against the mat when in truth the knees are meant to absorb the punishment—slammed Austin's head into the mat with more force than intended. How Austin managed to rouse himself to win in such pain is more than most of us can even imagine.

Austin spoke about injuries and accidents with a reporter from *The Dallas Morning News*, in a story dated December 13, 1998. He explained that as he was injured, he thought about Christopher Reeve, who had recently been paralyzed in an equestrian accident. "I thought I was paralyzed," Austin said. "I didn't think I was going to move again."

When it was revealed that his spinal cord was bruised and that he suffered stingers in both shoulders, he was sidelined for three months, and during that time he considered retirement. But then the Rattlesnake realized that nothing else could compare to a career in the ring. In the

December 5–11, 1998, issue of *TV Guide*, Austin talked about the future, and he realized that he needed to come back. "There's nothing like being in front of 15,000 to 20,000 people," he said. "It's a pure adrenaline rush. I like being in front of people."

So when he was healed up, he came back. "I started going to different doctors," he told dallasnews.com. "Never did one release me one hundred percent to go back, and none ever will. I wanted to return to the ring. I tested it and felt fine. I saw one doctor and he told me that if I felt fine and wasn't having any trouble, then go ahead." But ever since that incident with Owen Hart, Austin has refused to allow anyone to perform the pile driver on him. And he was not happy when this horrible reality he'd experienced was recreated as a one of the WWF's fictional plotlines, with Owen Hart giving Dan "the Beast" Severn a pile driver and then publicly regretting it.

"I don't believe any subject matter is sacred," he has said. "It's the American way." But that seemed over the line.

Austin is a rugged old wrestling veteran. He knows the way that world works. He understands that nothing should get in the way of the storyline. But that didn't mean he had to like it.

Outsiders not familiar with the ways of the wrestling world might think that no one could actually get hurt in the ring, because wrestling is fake—it's all rehearsed, right? Austin begs to differ about the risks and realities of wrestling.

"No, we don't really do any rehearsing, or stuff like that," he told reporters at a press conference promoting *SmackDown!* on UPN. "Going into a big show, or something like that, you've certainly got some ideas. But as many times as I've wrestled the Undertaker or the Rock, and I've seen them on film many times and watch them every night they work when we're on the road, I know what they do, and they pretty well know what I do. It's kind of like, you know, being a great musician, a magician. Going out there and creating something. The people don't know how you're doing it, but you're doing it. It just happens to be—you know, when you get at this level and being the best at what you do. You just go out there and it's just kind of like magic.

"But you have a few ideas and you might trade a few back and forth, but I've never had anybody say, 'Oh, yeah, let's go choreograph a match,' or, 'Here's some scripts. You go follow all these moves and we'll go out there and have a hell of a match.' You just go out there and you just kind of wing it.

"Basically, if I was to wrestle one of these guys out here, I'd be listening to a response. And if I'm absorbing that while I'm working, it's all psychology. You just don't go out there and beat each other up for the sake of beating each other up. It's psychology. . . . You're taking the crowd on a roller coaster ride up and down. And that's what it's all about."

And on that roller coaster, sometimes people get hurt. And all too often, Austin was one of those people. So as he continued to fight, the thoughts of retirement were always bubbling in his mind, but he kept pushing them away. He was also hobbled for a while by a torn abdominal muscle.

Austin didn't look good when he appeared at SummerSlam on August 22, 1999, wearing two stiff knee braces. Once the event was over, he announced that he would follow the program his doctors had been trying to get him to do for years—it was time for a rest. Perhaps he wouldn't listen to the doctors, but he listened to his body. August 22 was an eventful night, as many records were broken—Jeff Jarrett became the first six-time WWF Intercontinental Champion, D'Lo Brown became the first champion to lose two championships in one night, and it was the first time that the world title, the Intercontinental title, and the tag-team titles changed hands in a single night. But this was all secondary to the events that affected Steve Austin. When he lost the world title to Mankind that night, that sad news told him it was time to take a break.

Austin's decision regarding his injuries was considered so newsworthy that when *SmackDown!* debuted on August 26, 1999, it included a pretaped interview with Austin about his injuries.

But even though he wasn't wrestling per se, he did make appearances in the ring—just not as the unstoppable brawler. His rapport with the crowd was so great that the WWF had to come up with other roles for him. During the period of his injury, his role shifted to one that involved less active battling, but still kept him with a large onscreen presence. At the Unforgiven pay per view in Charlotte, North Carolina, at the Charlotte Coliseum on September 26, 1999, for example, he acted as a troubleshooting referee.

He was brought in as the enforcer at a Six-Pack Challenge match with the Rock vs. Mankind vs. the British Bulldog vs. Kane vs. the Big Show vs. Triple H for the world heavyweight title. This conglomeration of talent in the ring at the same time made for a strange event, but what was occurring outside made it even stranger. The WWF referees had decided to go out on strike, and were shown marching around the arena with picket signs. This meant that Austin had to be called into service to make sure there was order. But order is usually the furthest thing from the Rattlesnake's mind. The crowd roared when Austin leapt atop the announcer's table and held his hands in the air the same way he normally did at the turnbuckles. It was like putting a hungry fox in charge of the henhouse.

It was more a brawl than a match. And the striking referees took part in that brawl when they entered the arena to attack the scab who was officiating. Austin had to come to the defense of the poor scab, and then act as referee himself. When Austin finally made the three count and handed the belt over to the winning Triple H, the foolish Helmsley unfortunately took the opportunity to talk back to the Rattlesnake and taunt him with the belt. Triple H ended up on the mat, even though a winner—Austin gave him the Stunner for his troubles.

Then, on the October 11, 1999, *RAW Is WAR*, he teamed up with announcer Jim Ross to face Chyna and Triple H at Atlanta's Georgia Dome. It wasn't working for him, though. The pain was getting to be too much.

Austin tried to go on, but he was in such bad shape that he had to be scratched from the

November 14, 1999, Survivor Series. He was supposed to have participated in a triple-threat match with the Rock and Triple H. Whenever a star has to be cut from a bill, there's trouble, but he couldn't ignore his aggravated neck injury any longer.

The WWF did not announce his condition prior to that night, so that the pay-per-view sales would not be dampened. Vince McMahon had to do some quick thinking. The storyline the public was shown had Austin slammed into by a car in the parking lot of the Joe Louis Arena and then hospitalized. Since the Rattlesnake was unable to wrestle, the giant named Paul Wight aka the Big Show went on in his stead, going on to win the world heavyweight title.

So instead of grappling, Austin checked himself into the hospital on November 19, and not because of a fictitious car crash, but rather in an attempt to discover the extent of his injuries. He was told that his problems were severe. The pain he'd been feeling was caused by a bone spur touching his spinal cord, causing a numbness in his limbs.

On January 17, 2000, Austin underwent a four-hour-long operation on his neck to remove those bone spurs. He had confidence. He was to be in the care of Dr. Joseph Targ, the same physician who had cared for him during the Hart fiasco, with the operation overseen by Dr. Lloyd Youngblood.

Two days later, on January 19, 2000, Austin checked out of San Antonio's Methodist Hospital. He went on to recuperate at his home, where it would be an estimated six months before he could step back in the ring. After his neck has been immobilized for six weeks, he's scheduled to undergo further testing to see whether there was any permanent damage. Said Jim Byrne, a WWF spokesman, "We welcome Steve back in action the moment he's ready." Fans hoped that he would appear at the April 2 WrestleMania—for after four years of superb showings, what was WrestleMania without Austin?—but it was unlikely that he would recover by then.

But when he does recover, Austin's neck will be even stronger than it was before the operation, which should give hope to fans. According to hospital spokesperson JoAnn King-Sinnett, "Now he has metal in his neck." So Austin has become the man of steel.

"I think I will always be associated with the WWF in some capacity," Austin said during a cyber-chat on AOL just prior to the 1999 Royal Rumble, as he was considering his future. "Will I be able to wrestle forever? Of course not. But to me, being a part of the WWF is something special. And to me, I just like being associated with it."

Austin is so important to the WWF even in this condition that he was even scheduled against the Super Bowl. During the half-time show, viewers who changed channels to the USA Network saw a side of Austin they hadn't been privileged to witness before. He was seen relaxing at home thirteen days after his operation, beer in hand, talking to Jim Ross.

Austin removed his neck brace to show the scar on his throat and laughed off the pain. He complained that his only problem with what he'd endured was that the brace interfered with his beer drinking. He claimed to feel fine, and assured his many fans that he "ain't through yet." Once his bones were fused together properly, he insisted that he would be back, raising as much hell as ever.

"There ain't no way but a hundred percent for me," he said.

Ross wondered if that was wise, since Austin already had all the money and fame he could possibly want, but Austin discounted the risk. Staying at home and catching catfish was not enough of a thrill for him. He needed the charge that only came from performing. He remembers, following his first injury, when doctors told him to give up. His career since that time showed that they were wrong then, and they could be wrong now. Besides, there are no guarantees in this life, and Austin knew he could just as easily get hit by a car getting a newspaper. If he was going to go out, he wanted to do it in the ring.

And not least of all, he said threateningly, he had plenty of unfinished business with the Rock and Triple H.

And knowing Austin, they'd better watch out!

chapter 13

Tomorrow Never Dies

The future for this WWF champion is clear: Austin's fame, popularity, and riches will only continue to grow. The only question that remains for debate is in which arena he will decide to pursue these goals. Will he be returning to the ring as great as he ever was? Or will his injuries mean that his new arena will have to be the entertainment world? At the time of this writing, the direction of that future is uncertain. But the will of his fans and peers is unwavering—they want the Rattlesnake back!

Each of these two groups has a different reason for this desire. The fans want to be entertained. They know that Austin can deliver the goods as no one else can. And as for the other wrestlers, well, they, too, feel they have scores to settle. Austin isn't the only one with a long memory. When he gets back to the ring, there will be plenty of people waiting to outdo him. Mark

Calloway, aka the Undertaker, made some serious threats in regards to his rivalry with Austin.

"I'm not interested in proving my physical superiority over Steve Austin's puny body," he has said. "I am six-nine and 300 pounds of hell fury. I have nothing to accomplish by pinning Austin's shoulders in an athletic contest. I want him to lose hope and the will to survive."

And even those who have no such dark intent realize that the only one to best measure themselves against is Austin. If they don't have the Rattlesnake as a yardstick, how will they know they're any good?

The Rattlesnake continues to have the respect of his peers. Taz, the ECW champion who has recently jumped ship to join the WWF, has spoken publicly of his feelings about Austin. The wrestler, who now finds himself renamed as Tazz in the new federation, has also suffered an injured neck and thus can sympathize with the difficulties Austin faces in returning to the ring.

"Steve Austin and I are both nonconformist types," he said to a reporter from *WOW* magazine. "He doesn't stand by his company and run around with a WWF shirt. I think a lot of the stuff the WWF put in the character of Steve Austin was taken from what the ECW did with Taz. He is in the war alone."

Even the Rock has gone on record as being a fan of Austin's. When the People's Champion was asked by *Body Slam* magazine who his favorite wrestlers to work with were, his answer was clear. "Stone Cold, obviously, would be one," he said. "There's a certain chemistry there that's an intangible. People see that in our work; people see that type of magic in any match we have."

But will that magic have a chance to come again? In the December 5–11, 1998, issue of *TV Guide,* Austin talked about the future, which was obviously much on his mind even back then. "When I'm done with this, I'd like to try some Hollywood acting," he said. But the fans don't want Austin to be done with wrestling anytime soon. He is watched by more young men each Monday night than watch football, and they need their weekly dose of whup-ass.

With his choices so open between the worlds of wrestling and entertainment, one arena in which Austin is not interested is public office. He has no plans to be the next wrestler turned politician turned statesman, à la Jesse Ventura or Jerry Lawler.

"I'm really not into politics in any way, shape, or form as far as running for them," he has said. "But I've enjoyed some of the speeches Clinton's done, and with Jesse Ventura's election for

Minnesota governor, I think—I've always enjoyed listening to Jesse speak when he used to be here in the World Wrestling Federation, and as a broadcaster. I've followed him a little bit. But as far as myself involved—not at all."

In an election year, that is particularly disappointing. While the pundits delight in pointing out that the political arena is a bit too wild, some of us believe it would benefit by being a bit more like wrestling. If only Steve Austin would open a can of whup-ass in the White House, then things might get better!

No, it's clear that if Austin has his way, he'll be grappling again real soon. Talking to the editors of *Pro Wrestling Illustrated* after grabbing the top spot on their Top 500, Austin was quite clear that he shouldn't be written off yet. "I'm the best damn WWF champ ever," he said, "and on the verge of becoming the greatest wrestler of all time. You think winning two years in a row was a big deal? Try the next four or five at least."

Hopefully his body will let him achieve that goal. Unfortunately, most fear that his injuries will likely keep him from demonstrating the technical excellence that could give him the third consecutive slot in 2000, but he certainly has the top slot in the hearts of the fans.

As for his own top slot, he's stated that his

toughest opponent was Ricky "the Dragon" Steamboat. "The guy was just so good," Austin has said. "He never got tired. As far as here in the WWF, it would be a toss-up between Undertaker and Mankind."

If anyone tries to tell you that wrestling has hit its peak, don't believe them. It still has new untouched heights ahead of it. Wrestler biographies are hitting the bestseller lists, shoving Pulitzer-prize-winning authors out of the way. If television broadcasters had their way, they'd be running wrestling twenty-four hours a day.

And riding the crest of all of this popularity is Stone Cold Steve Austin, who has always given the fans 110 percent.

"I got a lot of respect for this damn WWF title, because a lot of the men that wore it before me earned my respect," he has said. "I want to give these people and the other wrestlers a champion they know will fight his heart and guts out every time he hits that damn ring. And as long as I can do that, I've won—I've beaten McMahon and his little jackass cronies."

As long as there are bosses who need to get their lights punched out, we will have a need for Austin. Whether he's in the ring or on the screen, he is alive in all of us, telling us that we don't have to take any crap from anyone. For those who are not happy with Austin's attitude, he has few words. "For anybody that can sit there on a high horse and knock what I do," he told *Newsweek*, "they can just piss off. This is wrestling. Take it for what it is."

Fans worry, though, that when he returns to the ring, he just won't be the same. But the fans might be surprised to discover that they're not the only ones who worry.

Austin worries, too.

"As a wrestler, I've learned to plan for any inevitability," he told Liz Hunter in *Inside Wrestling* magazine. "I've learned a long time ago that anything can happen in the course of a match. Am I prepared to lose? Hell, anything can happen."

Well, not quite anything.

On February 19, 1999, the WCW wrestler Bill Goldberg issued a challenge to Steve Austin that politics will prevent the Rattlesnake from ever picking up on. Goldberg appeared on *The Tonight Show with Jay Leno* and made a very public challenge to the WWF's number-one man. He offered $100,000 as a prize if the competing federation's champion would meet him on the field of battle.

Austin scoffed at the offer. He explained that he didn't have the time to face Goldberg " 'cause I have better things to do in the WWF." He also saw it as a publicity ploy to help the trailing WCW in the ratings, and slammed that federation with a backhand when he said that the two superstars would wrestle "when Goldberg made it to the big leagues." Perhaps he's just a bit miffed at the offer, because many consider Goldberg simply the WCW's attempt to create their own Austin. Whatever Austin's true feelings, it is unlikely that Vince McMahon would ever allow such cross-federation competition.

So while wrestling fans might be dreaming about such an encounter between the two toughest guys in wrestling, we shouldn't hold our breaths.

But we are all breathless waiting for his return at the same Stone Cold time and same Stone Cold channel. And we tremble in anticipation not just for the future of Austin, but for the future of the WWF and the entire sport of wrestling as well.

What will happen should wrestling lose its top gun? "If it's not fun tomorrow, then I'll find something else to do," Austin has said. "I'm having a blast right now."

But what if the pain is such that it suddenly no longer is fun? Can the WWF survive without Austin? The hit to the pocketbook and the ratings would be monumental. Some years, Austin's T-shirt, selling for twenty dollars apiece, have accounted for almost half of the $500 million in merchandise that the WWF makes annually.

McMahon has said privately that he already has the next five years of Austin storylines plotted out, though we'll have to wait to see them play out ourselves. Future injuries might mess with the program, but we're sure that McMahon—marketing genius that he is—has planned for that eventuality.

No one can replace Austin. "I take what I do extremely seriously," he has said, and it shows. He is at the top of the game, looking down at all comers. He's wrestled everyone and been willing to do anything to climb to the top. And that climb has given him renown that he could never have dared hope for when he was a kid watching grown men grapple on TV. He knew in his heart that he could conquer the world of wrestling, and the fame that came from the rest of the world was just gravy.

When Stone Cold Steve Austin was asked, looking back at his long career, whether he would have made any different choices, taken any different paths, he said, "I wouldn't change a damn thing."

And neither would his many fans.

Austin 3:16 says, "I just whupped your ass."

But surprisingly, unlike any wrestler before him, he's managed to whup our hearts and minds as well.

How?

Simple!

Because Stone Cold Steve Austin said so!

How Well Do You Know the Rattlesnake?

1: The reason Steve Williams changed his name to Steve Austin was because there was already a Steve Williams in pro wrestling. Under what character name did that first man wrestle?

a) The Undertaker
b) Dr. Death
c) Kane
d) Golddust

2: What was Steve Austin's nickname when he worked with the WCW?

a) Sparking
b) Sensational
c) Super
d) Stunning

3: The young Steve Williams received a college scholarship to North Texas University for playing which sport?

a) Football
b) Track and Field
c) Wrestling
d) Swimming

4: In which country did Austin receive his triceps muscle injury that caused his contract to be cancelled by the WCW?

a) Germany
b) U.S.A.
c) Japan
d) Canada

5: While at the WCW, who was the tag-team partner with whom he was known as the Hollywood Blonds?

a) Ric Flair
b) Brian Pillman
c) Brian Knobs
d) Billy Gunn

6: Which wrestler has Steve Austin stated to be his toughest opponent?

a) The Rock
b) The Undertaker
c) Owen Hart
d) Ricky "the Dragon" Steamboat

7: At the 1999 Royal Rumble, where Steve Austin had the unenviable first spot, what wrestling personality entered the ring second?

a) Vince McMahon
b) The Rock
c) The Big Show
d) Chyna

8: Against which wrestler was Austin battling at SummerSlam when he realized it was time to take a break and have his injuries attended to?

a) Triple H
b) Kane
c) Mankind
d) The Undertaker

9: Steve Williams studied the sport of wrestling by attending which grappler's training school?

a) "Gentleman" Chris Adams
b) "Killer" Kowalski
c) Verne Langdon
d) "Exotic" Adrian Street

10: Which voluptuous ring personality is Steve Austin's current fiancée?

a) Debra
b) Sable
c) Ivory
d) Miss Kitty

11: Austin came up with the idea for his world-famous catchphrase "Austin 3:15 says I just whupped your ass" after a feud with what other wrestler?

a) The Undertaker
b) Ric Flair
c) Kane
d) Jake "the Snake" Roberts

12: What image does Stone Cold Steve Austin have tattooed on his calf?

a) An upraised middle finger
b) The state of Texas
c) A heart with his girlfriend's name
d) The name of his college

13: Austin and his wife arrived at the "Stone Cold" nickname after he was warned about eating what before it got cold?

a) A cup of tea
b) A steak
c) A hamburger
d) A slice of pizza

14: Which WrestleMania was the first in which Steve Austin participated?

a) WrestleMania X
b) WrestleMania XI
c) WrestleMania XII
d) WrestleMania XIII

15: On the television show *Nash Bridges*, starring Don Johnson, what is the name of the character portrayed by Steve Austin?

a) Luke Cage
b) Jake Cage
c) Jake Fury
d) Steve Austin

16: Austin's signature finishing move, the Stone Cold Stunner, was adapted from which classic wrestling move?

a) The figure four leglock
b) The full nelson
c) The Pedigree
d) The Cobra Clutch

17: What is Steve Austin's beer of choice?

a) Coors Light
b) Budweiser
c) Michelob
d) Heineken

18: When Vince McMahon was hospitalized, with what object did Austin attack him?

a) An X-ray machine

b) A cafeteria tray
c) A bedpan
d) A hypodermic needle

19: For a brief period, who put Austin in charge of the WWF?

a) Gorilla Monsoon
b) Linda McMahon
c) Shane McMahon
d) Shawn Michaels

20: Whose interference allowed Steve Austin to win the St. Valentine's Day Massacre?

a) The Rock
b) Vince McMahon
c) Jim Ross
d) The Big Show

21: How many wrestlers did Steve Austin eliminate from competition at the 1999 Royal Rumble?

a) Eight
b) Seven
c) Ten
d) Twelve

22: During what year did Steve Austin wrestle in the ECW?

a) 1993
b) 1994
c) 1995
d) 1996

23: Steve Austin's loss to which wrestler caused Ted DiBiase to leave the WWF?

a) Brian Pillman
b) Savio Vega
c) Jake "the Snake" Roberts
d) Golddust

24: Who was Austin fighting during an Intercontinental title match when he was injured by a pile driver?

a) Owen Hart
b) Triple H
c) The Rock
d) Mike Tyson

25: Who was Austin's opponent for a steel cage match at the 1999 St. Valentine's Day Massacre?

a) Cactus Jack
b) Triple H
c) The Undertaker
d) Vince McMahon

Answers:

1-B, 2-D, 3-A, 4-C, 5-B, 6-D, 7-A, 8-C, 9-A, 10-A, 11-D, 12-B, 13-A, 14-C, 15-B, 16-D, 17-A, 18-C, 19-B, 20-D, 21-A, 22-C, 23-B, 24-A, 25-D

If you got 25 correct: Congratulations! You're qualified to take over the WWF from Vince McMahon! Move over, Shane and Stephanie!

If you got 20 correct: Good for you! Perhaps you should send your résumé to the WWF and take over Jim Ross's job.

If you got 15 correct: You'd better open that wallet and try watching a few more pay per views.

If you got only 10 correct: Uh-oh. Better stay home on Monday night more often and keep your eyes glued to *RAW Is WAR*.

If you got fewer than 5 correct: Are you sure you've ever seen a wrestling match?

25. Who was Austin's opponent for a steel cage match at the 1998 St. Valentine's Day Massacre?
a) Cactus Jack
b) Triple H
c) The Undertaker
d) Vince McMahon

Answers:
1-B 2-D 3-A 4-C 5-B 6-D 7-A 8-C 9-A
10-A 11-D 12-B 13-A 14-C 15-B 16-D 17-A
18-C 19-B 20-D 21-A 22-C 23-B 24-A 25-D

If you got 25 correct: Congratulations! You're qualified to take over the WWF from Vince McMahon! [illegible]

If you got 20 correct: [illegible] Perhaps you should send your résumé to the WWF and take over Jim Ross's job.

If you got 15 correct: It's a [illegible] wallet and try watching a [illegible]

If you got only 10 correct: [illegible] house on Monday night [illegible] and keep your eyes glued to RAW IS WAR.

If you got fewer than 5 correct: Are you sure you [illegible] wrestling [illegible]